C000173518

More a Way of Life

Also by Robert Cull

More to Life Than This

More a Way of Life

Further Stories of Jean Cull,
the medium

Robert Cull

MACMILLAN
LONDON

Photographs by Marcus Wilson-Smith

Copyright © Robert Cull 1988

All rights reserved. No reproduction, copy or transmission of
this publication may be made without written permission. No
paragraph of this publication may be reproduced, copied or
transmitted save with written permission or in accordance
with the provisions of the Copyright Act 1956 (as amended).
Any person who does any unauthorised act in relation to this
publication may be liable to criminal prosecution and civil
claims for damages.

First published 1988 by
MACMILLAN LONDON LIMITED
4 Little Essex Street, London WC2R 3LF
and Basingstoke

Associated companies in Auckland, Delhi, Dublin,
Gaborone, Hamburg, Harare, Hong Kong, Johannesburg,
Kuala Lumpur, Lagos, Manzini, Melbourne, Mexico City,
Nairobi, New York, Singapore and Tokyo

British Library Cataloguing in Publication Data

Cull, Robert
  More a way of life.
  I. Spiritualism. Mediums: Cull, Jean –
  Biographies
  I. Title
  133.9′1′0924

ISBN 0-333-48201-8

Typeset by Rowland Phototypesetting Limited
Bury St Edmunds, Suffolk
Printed in Great Britain by Richard Clay Limited
Bungay, Suffolk

This book is for you, Gran.
'You are only a thought away.'

Contents

Contents

Acknowledgement

Special thanks to Tom Weldon, my editor, for all his help and advice with my first book and especially with this one.

Introduction

In my first book, *More To Life Than This*, I gave a full account of how Jean and I were led into the fascinating world of mediumship and psychic phenomena. We were directed and guided by a group of spirit people whom we now regard as our closest friends. A plan was contrived by this group of spirit friends led by Henry and Lucy to change my scepticism to conviction, and to persuade Jean to develop her natural gift and train to become a full-time professional medium.

When we discovered that Jean had been born with this natural ability to 'see' and 'talk' to spirit people, our whole way of life was changed. After years of training and development Jean now works as a professional medium, bringing comfort and joy to thousands of people. We now understand that Jean's natural gift as a medium was meant to be shared with as many people as possible. Jean achieves this by giving public demonstrations and private sittings whenever and wherever she is invited to do so.

This book is the continuing story of Jean's life as a medium, a life that is dedicated to the alleviation of the anxiety and sadness which often follow bereavement. Jean proves through the gift of mediumship that there is no death, that loved ones who pass from this earthly life are not lost for ever; they live on in the spirit world and, should they choose, can communicate with us through the channel of a medium. Jean is this channel. She is the link with the spirit world, a link which reunites loved ones, reawakens old friendships and cements new ones.

It is not, as some people claim, a frightening experience to be reunited with a loved one from the spirit world. Anyone who has had a sitting with Jean will confirm this. Jean shares her gift with love, sincerity and total dedication. Whenever we hear or read of anyone who treats the subject with disrespect, or of a medium or so-called medium upsetting or frightening people, we take steps to stop this despicable behaviour if we possibly can.

However, there is a side to Jean's mediumship that the general public has never seen and never will, and it can be frightening and dangerous. I will describe in detail how Jean and her spirit friends help the 'lost souls' who wander in the darker planes of the spirit world, and how Jean came face to face with the evil power that exists in the darker side of spirit. She was rescued from this ordeal by her friends in spirit, but it has left her with an unforgettable memory, a memory that prompts us always to warn people of the dangers of dabbling with psychic forces.

This sequel to *More To Life Than This* is not simply a catalogue of the private sittings or public demonstrations which Jean has given over the years. I have attempted to give a broad and complete picture of life in the spirit world. By selecting examples of how Jean has helped people in a variety of ways, I hope to help those who feel they have similar problems. I explain the detailed and long preparation undertaken by Jean before any demonstration of mediumship. What actually takes place during a private sitting? How does Jean receive the messages? What is she doing that the sitter is unaware of? These and many more questions will be answered in the book. With her spirit friends Jean has advised and guided many business people in their work, she helps those who are being troubled by spirits in their homes, she has offered information she received from spirit to the police. There are lots of amusing anecdotes in the book.

I hope that by sharing our experiences we may encourage those seeking the truth of life after death to continue with their search. Those who feel they would benefit from the services of a medium but feel afraid to seek them may be helped to make the decision. To those who are still mourning the loss of a loved one or a friend, I hope my book may give you comfort and reassurance that your loved ones are not lost to you for ever; they do live on and are as close to you now as ever they were in the body. If you feel that you have been blessed with a special gift, Jean's example may inspire you to consider developing your gift and sharing it with others.

It will become apparent to you as you read my book how seriously Jean and I regard our involvement with spirit. Jean has said many times that her life as a medium is not simply a way of earning a living. She has dedicated her life to improving and perfecting the means of communication between our world and the spirit world. She is now fulfilling her destiny. She knows at last why she was born with her special gifts, for her spirit friends have led her to the life she now leads. Jean's mediumship is no longer her privately guarded secret; to both of us it is 'more a way of life'.

Chapter One

Only a Thought Away

The man looked embarrassed as Jean led him into the kitchen from the sitting room. It was obvious he had been crying.

Jean smiled at the other man who had been waiting to see her. 'Hello, I'm Jean,' she said with a smile as she walked over and shook his hand. 'Would you like to come through now? I'm sorry we are running a little late but it's impossible always to keep to a strict time schedule.' Jean left the kitchen still chattering away to the other man.

I smiled sympathetically at his friend who was now seated at the table. They had come together to see Jean. 'Would you like a cup of tea or coffee?' I asked.

'Coffee, please,' he answered between sniffs. 'You must excuse me,' he continued, 'but it was absolutely incredible. I just can't believe it.' I said there was no need for apologies as I had seen the same reaction from people after their sittings a thousand times. When I mentioned that I had seen as many men as women enter the kitchen in the same emotional state, I sensed his embarrassment ease. I said it was pleasing to see such emotion as it usually indicated that the sitting had been a success. As I passed him his coffee he said he would like to listen to the recording of his sitting now that he had calmed down a little. He invited me to listen with him while he waited for his friend. 'You will see just how successful the sitting was,' he said, this time with a smile.

I took his cassette and placed it in the recorder I keep in the kitchen (his friend was recording his sitting on their own machine). Jean's voice could be heard loud and clear as she asked the familiar question that normally begins most sittings. 'Have you ever had a sitting with a medium before?' The man replied that this was his first time.

'That's fine, just relax. I can assure you nothing strange is going to happen. You will not hear any strange voices or see anything unusual. I will simply be talking to you. First I need to hold something that you wear regularly: your watch or ring, for example. I promise you will get it back.' There was a short pause, then Jean continued. 'You haven't been sleeping well lately and you have been experiencing headaches. Both of these conditions are very unusual for you. You have a headache at the moment, haven't you?'

The man said Jean was absolutely right, he had not slept well for ages and had been suffering from headaches. He agreed that it was very unusual for him as he normally slept like a baby and had never had headaches before.

'You've had a serious argument recently – no, wait a moment, it was today. It has something to do with your work. You haven't handed your notice in today, have you, for I feel that would have been a mistake. You will receive an apology in the next few days, so don't worry.'

The man replied that it was amazing, he had indeed had a serious row with his boss and was considering handing in his notice.

'You are very worried about a change that has taken place in your life. This change has nothing to do with a work situation, this is to do with a relationship that you are not sure about. This worry that you have about the friendship is linked with something that happened to you a few years ago.'

The man agreed, saying this was the reason for him making the appointment to see Jean.

Jean then handed back the man's watch, saying she no longer needed it. Her voice changed to a much softer and gentler tone. 'If I was to talk to you of someone who has passed on, would this worry or frighten you in any way?'

The man said he didn't think it would.

'Good, for a young lady has drawn very close to you and she is giving me the feeling that she was your wife. I've just heard the name David.'

The man said his name was David.

'You also know the name Judith.'

The man replied that his wife's name had been Judith.

Jean then described the young lady and added that she was standing between Jean and David. 'Sadly your wife was not as I see her now when she passed. I get the feeling of a long and painful illness. She passed with cancer, didn't she?'

David in a very emotional voice said yes, his wife had died of cancer.

'I assure you your wife is no longer in pain, she is happy and well and full of life. I see her exactly as she is now, pretty, happy and full of life. She's smiling and tells me the watch was a birthday present. Your birthday is very soon. Judith sends her love for your birthday.'

In a very quiet voice, and with a distinct tremor, David said that his wife had bought the watch for his birthday. He said his birthday was in two weeks' time.

Jean continued with some personal details about David and his wife, and then made what seemed a very casual remark which produced a dramatic reaction from David. 'Judith is very happy for you, she says she likes Lynne.'

David broke down completely and wept unashamedly. I could hear him saying over and over again, 'Oh my God, oh my God.' Jean passed him the tissues which are always in plentiful supply during a sitting. After a few minutes David composed himself and apologised for his outburst. Jean said in a very understanding voice that she was so pleased to see his emotion and he had no cause to apologise. David then went on

3

to explain why he was so moved. He had met Lynne about a year ago and they had been seeing each other regularly since. They had enjoyed each other's company and recently the relationship had deepened and they both felt that they wanted to become engaged. David was very worried about how his wife Judith might feel towards this new relationship. He said he felt guilty because he and Judith had been so happy and very much in love. He was concerned that she might not approve, and that if she knew how he felt about Lynne it might make her unhappy. Jean said that Judith was saying how happy she was for David that he was at last beginning to lead a normal life again, and that she gave him and Lynne her blessing and her love.

David then asked Jean a question that is often asked at discussion groups or by people who have been married twice. 'Jean, if Lynne and I do get married, what will happen when we all meet up in the spirit world?'

Jean explained that David should now know how pleased Judith was about the new relationship he had with Lynne. 'If a person has married more than once and there was a truly loving relationship between them, when the husbands or wives meet in the spirit world the love they had for each other will unite them. In your case, David, Judith loved you very much, as does Lynne, so there is a natural love between the three of you. When the time comes and you are all in the spirit world, this love will blend together and form a common factor between you. There will be a spiritual love between you that will strengthen the bond and bring you all closer together.' Jean added that if there was any jealousy or ill-feeling between couples in these circumstances, then there would be a separation in the spirit world. 'You will only meet those you love or those who loved you. You have nothing to worry about.'

As David and I sat listening to the recording I could see the tears welling up once again in David's eyes. I hoped he would be able to control his emotions, for I knew that if he should let go once again I myself would find it difficult to hold back my emotion for him. I said what a marvellous message he had received from his wife, and how relieved he must be feeling now that he knew he had Judith's blessing on his new-found relationship. I told him that his wife must have been a very understanding person, and that her love for him still came through. David said Jean would never know how much she had helped him, for the feeling of guilt he had had would always have caused a problem between him and Lynne. I replied that I knew how pleased Jean would be to have linked with Judith, and to have been able to pass on her love and support to David.

Jean came into the kitchen shortly afterwards with David's friend. 'Are you feeling better now, David?' Jean asked. 'Just remember that Judith is happy and well and is still very close to you and still loves you very much.'

David stood up and in a spontaneous gesture threw his arms round Jean and hugged her. 'You'll never know what you have done for me tonight, Jean. I don't know how I could ever repay you,' he said.

'You just have,' Jean said with a smile. 'I'll let you into a secret. One of the reasons I decided to become a medium is because I get hugged and kissed by some lovely young men.' We all laughed as I led David and his friend to the door.

When I shook David's hand to say goodbye he smiled and said, 'You take good care of Jean, Bob, she's one in a million.' I promised him that I would.

This description of what David was experiencing before coming to see Jean, his worry and anxiety over the reaction his wife might have had to his new relationship, and what transpired during the sitting may offer comfort and reassurance to those who find themselves in a similar situation. We can learn two very important lessons from David's experience. First, that it is right and proper to mourn the loss of a loved one or a friend. No matter how strong a message from spirit may be, it cannot nor ever will replace the actual physical contact that has ended.

Spirit communication can never be a satisfactory substitute for physical contact. I will never forget how I felt after losing both my parents within six months of each other: I was devastated. However, my conviction that there is life after death helped me tremendously during the mourning period, and my understanding and acceptance of the spirit world made my recovery from the loss much quicker. We all have to realise after a bereavement that life must go on. It is not insensitive to find a new friendship or partner, provided that we remember our departed friends with love and respect. It is understandable to feel that in forming new relationships we might be acting disloyally to a husband or wife who has passed on, but in fact it is simply an expression of the love we have for them. This leads to the second lesson we can learn from David's sitting.

Loved ones and friends in the spirit world are always happy to see that we are continuing to enjoy life. Of course they know and understand how much we miss them and are touched by our sorrow and distress at their passing. It is when our mourning extends beyond the 'normal' that they become concerned for us, and then we make them unhappy. Jean has passed on hundreds of messages from loved ones in the spirit world asking relatives to stop mourning and start to enjoy life. When we are happy in our life, our spirit friends are happy with us; when we are sad and unhappy they too feel sad and unhappy. Always remember that your loved ones are 'only a thought away' – they are as close to you now as ever they were. When they lived with you in the physical body, they reacted to your various moods. You shared your happiness with them and they responded by being happy for you. When you were sad, they too felt sad. Nothing has changed, even though you may not see or hear them. Continue to share your life with them, for they are still close to you. Remember the happy times, talk to your loved ones exactly as you used to do; they love to hear your voice. You do not have to be a medium to sense and feel their response. I promise you that if you still act as if they are with you in the body, *you will feel their presence*.

Many people who come to see Jean for a private sitting are visiting a medium for the first time. They may have strange ideas about what will happen. Because of Jean's relaxed and casual manner during a sitting it might appear that she is doing very little indeed. The sitter has no indication of the work that is being done behind the scenes by Jean and her spirit friends who help her. To give some idea of just what does happen, I will analyse David's sitting, and explain exactly what took place and how Jean received the communication that followed. This will also give the inexperienced an insight into the preparation that is needed beforehand to enable Jean to receive communication from the spirit world.

Jean's preparation for a sitting begins at least two hours before the appointed time. She begins to withdraw into herself, and I can see and sense that her mind is elsewhere. It becomes increasingly difficult to hold a conversation with her, for her replies are purely automatic and given without due thought. In many instances she won't hear me at all. Having lived with this for many years, I now accept and understand what is happening. I no longer react to this feeling of being shut out or ignored, for I know how important this preparation is. If we are booked for a public meeting and I too am required to speak or give an address, this solitude within our own thoughts becomes mutual. You can imagine how quiet our house becomes during this preparation stage. Our son Andrew is very considerate and is well aware of what is happening, so he leaves us both well alone in our own thoughts. A stranger who did not understand what was going on would think we were very unsociable and a miserable family who never speak to each other.

Jean's preparation is far more concentrated and critical than mine. If any friends are coming to a public meeting taken by Jean and me, they always agree to meet us after the meeting has finished. They are aware of Jean's need for privacy before she demonstrates. On the occasions when it has been necessary to travel to a meeting with friends, they have respected Jean's needs. She has some special music cassettes that she likes to listen to just prior to working, and on the journey she will sit silently in the back of the car listening to her music, while I and the other friends talk very quietly together. Usually we find that as we get near to the venue for the meeting we all stop talking and sit in silence. Again it must seem rather odd to outsiders to see four friends sitting in a car and not talking to each other. We are always appreciative of the consideration shown by our friends in these circumstances.

When Jean is preparing for a private sitting at home, she will take a bath about an hour before the sitters arrive. Then she gets dressed and does her hair and make-up. About half an hour before the sitting she completely secludes herself from everybody, locking herself away in the bedroom. Now she moves into top gear for her preparation. I busy myself checking that the cups and saucers are in place and there is enough tea and coffee on hand. If there is more than one sitter coming, I put out some books or magazines for them to read while they are waiting to see Jean. I check the diary to refresh my memory on the names of the expected sitters. When all is in order I wait until I hear Jean come down from the bedroom to the sitting room, which will also have been shut up for the last half-hour. I take her a glass of orange juice and ask if she is ready. She either simply nods her head or says yes.

What has Jean been doing for that half-hour locked away in the bedroom? Having already begun to withdraw into herself, she must now begin the process of linking with the spirit world. To begin with she needs to clear her mind completely of her own thoughts of home, family, and all the concerns of this earthly life. She must try to prevent any mundane thoughts from intruding. If you have ever tried to clear your mind of thoughts, you will understand just how difficult this exercise can be. Part of the training Jean received when developing her mediumship was the technique that enables her to achieve a clear mind.

Once Jean has relaxed and is in this receptive mental state she then opens her mind to her friends in spirit. As Henry and

Lucy are always very close, this is the first 'contact' she makes. She needs to know that they are in attendance, as she would be unable to work in any way with spirit without their help. Henry is the leader of this team of spirit friends, and his role is the most important. It is his responsibility to organise all that takes place whenever Jean is demonstrating, and he monitors and supervises the proceedings in an orderly fashion. Without his supervision the result could be total confusion.

As you can imagine, the number of loved ones in the spirit world eager to communicate with relatives and friends at any one time is incalculable. If Jean opened up her mediumistic ability without Henry's control, she would be completely swamped by voices and messages to pass on. We have all experienced being talked to by several people at the same time: the result is confusion, and it is very difficult to understand anything that is being said. If you magnify this a thousand times, you will appreciate the chaos that would ensue. Henry controls this situation by allowing only one communicator to speak at a time. When Jean is satisfied that Henry and Lucy are near and have things under control, she asks Henry to tell those who may choose to communicate to do so clearly, precisely, and to the very best of their ability. Jean is now ready to come down to the sitting room and await the arrival of her first sitter.

So let us follow the sitting of David and his friend. When they arrived I took them into the kitchen and offered them coffee. Having asked who had chosen to see Jean first, I took David through to the sitting room and introduced him to Jean. I explained to Jean that David had brought a tape recorder, and then I closed the door and returned to the kitchen to keep David's friend company.

Jean showed David where to sit and then plugged in the tape recorder and tested that the machine was functioning properly. That done she settled herself into her favourite chair. The sitting was ready to commence. At this stage Jean is in such a highly sensitive state because of her preparation that she can

9

immediately sense any nerves or apprehension coming from the sitter. David was obviously nervous, so Jean's first priority was to try to calm his nerves and get him to relax. This is important, as it helps to create a friendly and harmonious atmosphere which spirit will respond to. Jean will sometimes spend five to ten minutes simply talking and calming the sitter, and never begins the sitting until she is happy that the sitter is relaxed and responsive to the possibility of spirit communication.

Having calmed David and felt that he was ready to begin, Jean asked if she might hold his watch. In most sittings this is her first request. This is very important, for as well as being a medium Jean is also a 'psychometrist'. By simply holding an object that a person has worn or wears regularly, she is able to sense and receive a great deal of information relating to its owner. It is this faculty which some mediums possess that the police use to help them with certain enquiries. (I will give examples later in the book of information Jean has supplied to the police using psychometry and her other gifts.)

Holding David's watch, Jean was very quickly able to discover the sort of person he was. She can sense what has happened to the person and also what is happening at the time. She has described the sensation by saying, 'It's as if I *become* those people. I feel their moods, what's worrying them. I take on all their emotions.' David had been a complete stranger to Jean when he was introduced, but by simply holding his watch she now knew exactly the sort of person she was sitting with. How is this possible?

The human body is enveloped by what is called an 'aura'. This electromagnetic energy field can supply a psychometrist with information on the health and physical state of the person. The mental aura conveys the mental state of the person, his or her character and personality. The 'soul' or spiritual aura can tell a sensitive observer the degree of spiritual development an individual may have attained. In simple terms, surrounding us all is a rainbow that vibrates and changes in colour and intensity according to our health, mood, personality and spiritual understanding. People like Jean can sometimes actually see this energy field around us, but can *always* sense its presence. If we regularly wear an object such as a watch, a ring or a necklace, this object is constantly in contact with our aura and so subsequently absorbs it. When Jean holds the object she can sense and feel details relating to the owner.

In David's case Jean was able to sense the headaches and the sleep problem. She knew about the argument at work and the change that had taken place in a personal relationship, and how worry about this was linked to a particular event some years previously. It is important to emphasise that the information Jean receives from this source has nothing to do with spirit communication, it is purely a psychic faculty that she possesses. The information comes from the object and not from spirit. Jean needs to make this very personal contact with the sitter before she begins her work as a medium. As I have explained, she has already made her link with her spirit friends before the sitter's arrival; she now needs to form a three-way link between herself, the sitter, and finally spirit. By forming this close relationship with the sitter she draws him into the triangle, bringing him into closer contact with spirit. This need for a close link between the medium, the sitter and spirit explains why at a public meeting Jean always asks for a loud positive response from the person she is directed to. At a public meeting the voice is the only thing she receives from that person, so she needs to use his or her response to form the triangle. Jean hates what she terms the 'nodders', the people who simply nod or shake their heads. If you phoned a friend and he simply nodded or shook his head in response to what you said, you can imagine how impossible it would be to continue the conversation. Jean has often described her role as a medium as being the instrument (the telephone) linking the spirit world to our world. If the person receiving 'the call' does not respond, it makes her role that much more difficult.

In the circumstances of a private sitting, however, once Jean is satisfied that the triangle is complete and the psychometry has been accepted by the sitter, she hands the object back. She then switches off this purely psychic faculty and opens the door to the spirit world.

A medium does not call upon the spirit world. Whoever communicates with a sitter does so of his own free will. Jean has no control in the matter of who will or will not communicate. She cannot summon a relative or friend simply because the sitter would like to 'speak' to that individual. She has found that if there is a genuine need or reason for a particular communication, spirit usually does respond, but it should be stressed that this can never be guaranteed. We can never know the effort and work that take place in the spirit world to make communication possible. To a genuine medium this unknown factor will always give rise to a feeling of concern – is it going to work at any given time or not? In all the years that Jean has been acting as a medium, only twice has she received no communication at all, on both occasions at a private sitting. She could only apologise and explain that there was nothing she could do about it. With David, however, the sitting went well.

While Jean was holding the watch she became aware of a woman who had drawn close to her. She asked David if he would be upset if she spoke of spirit people, and when he said no, Jean handed the watch back to him and 'tuned into' the woman who had made her presence felt. She then passed on the information she received from Judith. Jean is a channel not only for communication but also for emotion. She can pass on the emotion of the spirit to the sitter, and vice versa. This is one of the reasons why she feels very tired after a demonstration or sitting, for she is being used as an emotional sponge.

Spirit are often reluctant to talk of their passing, but Jean could sense from Judith the manner in which she had passed to the spirit world. David was able to confirm Jean's feeling and explain how his wife had actually passed. Jean will always, as she did in David's case, reassure sitters that their loved ones are no longer in pain but are happy and well. Following more personal conversation between the sitter, spirit and herself, Jean will begin to sense spirit withdrawing. If no other spirit communicators make their presence felt, Jean knows the sitting is drawing to a close. She will now repeat any advice that may have been given from spirit, tie up any loose ends and generally sum up the sitting. She will ask if the sitter has any questions to ask: she never closes a sitting until she is satisfied that the sitter understands and is happy with what has transpired. She then escorts the sitter back to the kitchen.

When I hear the sitting-room door open it is always accompanied by the sound of Jean chattering away, usually on any subject other than spirit. She comes into the kitchen still chatting, and continues this casual conversation as she escorts the next sitter from the kitchen into the sitting room. This is a deliberate exercise which allows Jean, in the few minutes' break between sittings, to clear her mind of what has taken place during the previous session. Walking from the sitting room to the kitchen expresses by physical action the moving away from spirit. It is not until the sitter has settled down that Jean opens her mind once again and another sitting begins.

Chapter Two

Terror

As I have said in my introduction, there is a side to Jean's work as a medium that the general public has never seen and will never see, which can be frightening and upsetting. It demands courage from the mediums to allow themselves to be used by spirit for this particular aspect of mediumship, which we refer to as 'rescue work'. Jean was fortunate that the mediums who took charge of her training were familiar with this work and they encouraged and developed her ability to serve spirit in this field. Rescue work requires the total trust of the spirit friends who help the medium. Jean has earned this trust from her friends and it enables her to open her mind to the 'lower planes' of the spirit world, where rescue work is usually undertaken.

In order to understand rescue work fully, an explanation of the term 'lower planes' and the souls who dwell there is necessary. It is a sad fact that our world is a very violent place. Every day we read about or see on television acts of violence against other human beings. Some people seem to enjoy hurting or threatening others, and get pleasure from dominating those whose will is weaker than their own.

When a person dies it is only his or her physical body that is left behind. The spirit or soul separates from the physical body and begins its spiritual journey. The spirit is the *real* you:

your characteristics and personality are retained by your spirit on its transition to the spirit world. All your likes and dislikes, your true feelings go with you to the spirit world, shedding the façade that the physical body may have been. Our true individuality remains the same and intact, exactly as it was prior to death.

If a person had a vindictive nature, if he was jealous or enjoyed hurting and frightening others, his spirit will retain these traits. The personality does not suddenly change on arrival in the spirit world. We do not automatically become pious and humble; there is no miraculous transformation of character. Therefore, just as we accept that in their earthly life there are people who are not pleasant and kind, we must realise that it is the same in the spirit world.

There is a strong law of attraction evident in our earthly life. We tend to mix with people of like minds, enjoying the company of those with similar interests and hobbies. Our friends are people in whose company we feel safe and happy. Likewise criminals and villains prefer the company of those leading similar lives, in a community we term 'the underworld'. In the world of spirit this law of attraction is as strong as it is here. It draws spirits of similar temperament together according to their spirituality and understanding. We refer to these various groupings as the 'planes' of spirit. The deeper the understanding and spirituality, the higher the plane of existence. Disturbed, violent or vengeful spirits obviously occupy what we call the lower planes. The terms 'higher' and 'lower' are not literal, for the spirit world has no geographical location equivalent to the earth plane. It is not some far-off place like a planet or another world, but purely another conscious dimension. When we talk about 'lower plane' we merely imply that those who exist in this realm are nearer to the earth plane. They desire to remain close to the physical world and its material lifestyle. These people had little or no spiritual aspiration in their earthly life, and continue to feel the same in the spirit world.

When Jean chooses to communicate with those in the lower

planes she never knows whom she may meet. This is why she needs the protection of her spirit friends. It is vital that she can trust Henry to control and protect her as she offers herself to this dark area of the spirit world. Henry has always led the team of spirit friends who work to help Jean with her mediumship. Besides organising all the communication Jean receives from spirit, he also acts as her protector against undesirable influences from these darker planes. We describe Henry's role as Jean's 'doorkeeper', guarding her psychic door to the spirit world. When Jean is giving both private sittings and public demonstrations, it is important that she is not influenced or troubled by those from the lower planes. We could therefore more accurately call Henry her psychic bodyguard or bouncer.

If Jean wishes to link with the lower planes, this will, under the careful scrutiny of Henry, be allowed. Such a request is made so that we can try to offer help and guidance to those on the darker side of spirit, and perhaps encourage in them a more spiritual outlook. We try to rescue them, hence the term 'rescue work', from their insecurity and their fruitless wanderings as they cling to the memories of their physical life. There is also help at hand from the spirit world, for many souls in spirit move to the lower planes to offer guidance and counselling to those in need. We work in unison with these friends, and feel proud to have helped many souls to find a new and constructive awareness.

I believe that there is a power for good and for evil present in our world, both of them very potent. We can choose from either source, channelling this energy to harm or to help. If we pray for someone, we are channelling a power for the well-being of that person. If we reverse the process, then it is possible to hurt or injure someone. We should never underestimate the power of thought. A medium is the channel for spirit, and since there is also a power of good and evil in the spirit world the same choice is available. Those who get involved in black magic, satanism and the occult can channel this evil power from the spirit world. Only once has Jean experienced the evil power from the dark side of spirit; she described it as the most frightening event of her life. It did prove, however, the strength of the protection she receives from Henry and her team of spirit friends. This is how it occurred.

Jean had been very busy and felt tired, so a friend of ours called Jessie who lived in London invited us to spend a few days at her flat. Jessie was a long-standing friend of another medium whom Jean and I had read about and longed to meet. Leslie Flint was a famous 'direct voice'* medium who had been demonstrating his extraordinary gift for most of his life. The phenomenon of the direct voice mediumship is the ability of spirit to speak to the sitter totally independent of the medium. It requires a medium with very special powers to achieve the conditions necessary for this to take place. We were fortunate to have a sitting with Leslie just before he retired as a medium. Now Jessie had pulled a few strings and persuaded Leslie to come to lunch so that we could meet and talk to him. We were very excited at the prospect of meeting such a renowned medium.

Jean was still in the early years of her training and the children were very young. Jessie's invitation coincided with the school holidays, and Wendy said she would rather stay with her grandparents while Andrew said he would like to come with us. On our first day in London we took Andrew to see some of the sights, and spent the evening talking to Jessie, planning lunch and Leslie's visit the next day.

Leslie arrived at about midday. After a pleasant lunch we sat talking and exchanging experiences until late into the night. Andrew had visited Jessie's son during the afternoon and had spent a happy time playing with Jessie's grandchildren. When he came back it was time for him to go to bed. He mentioned to Jean that he hadn't slept too well the night before, so she said he could sleep in the other twin bed with her while I took

---

* A fuller explanation of this type of mediumship is described in my first book, *More To Life Than This*.

the single bed in the other room. By the time we finished talking, Andrew was fast asleep. We said our goodnights and I went into the single room. I was very tired and soon fell asleep, totally unaware of the terrifying experience Jean was about to witness in the next room.

I was the first awake the next morning. I got dressed and went quietly into the kitchen to make myself some coffee. Before I had finished my coffee Jean came into the kitchen looking very anxious. I asked her what was the matter. 'I have had the most frightening experience of my life,' she replied. Jean made me promise not to tell anyone what had happened during the night. She said she didn't want to upset Jessie or frighten Andrew. And then she told me what had taken place.

'I went into the room and checked that Andrew was asleep. I felt very tired and after saying my prayers I soon fell asleep. I woke in the early hours feeling most uncomfortable. I was soaked in perspiration yet I felt cold and was shivering. I lay still for a few minutes to clear my head and then looked to see if a window was open. All the windows were closed yet the room felt freezing. I tried to get out of bed to have a drink of water and wash my face. It was then that I realised I couldn't move. The more I tried to get up, the more I became aware of this pressure pinning me to the bed. I felt as if I were paralysed. I panicked and tried to call out to you, but I couldn't speak. I tried again to get out of bed using all my strength, but I was being held down and felt powerless against this unseen force. I forced myself to be rational and thought: This is stupid. Just relax and calm down and try to think this through.

'I lay still and found I could turn my head, but the rest of my body felt as if it were held in a vice. I looked over towards Andrew who was fast asleep and apparently totally oblivious of what was happening. As I lay back and closed my eyes I gradually became aware of an awful feeling that was growing in the room. I opened my eyes and looked round; I could sense this horrible presence but I could see nothing. I knew then that the presence was spirit. I heard nothing and could see nothing,

18

but it was a feeling I had never before experienced from spirit: *it was evil*. At the very moment that I became aware that it was linked to spirit, the pressure increased. I could feel myself being forced deeper and deeper into the bed, as if something were trying to push me through it. I tried with all my strength to resist this pressure but I felt like a new-laid egg under the wheel of a steamroller. During my struggle I again looked over at Andrew and in my mind sent out the thought, "Please don't let it touch him." It was becoming difficult to breathe; I was being suffocated. For the first time in my life I thought I was going to die, and my thoughts turned to my friends in spirit. "Henry, please help me. If there is anything you can do, please do it."

'I still found it difficult to breathe but the pressure did not increase. I sensed what I can only describe as a conflict taking place. Gradually I felt the pressure beginning to ease and was soon able to take some deep breaths. Eventually I was able to sit up in bed and the horrible feeling began to fade. I lay back feeling exhausted and frightened. Then I got up and went over to Andrew, who was sleeping undisturbed and looked very peaceful. I stood looking round the room; the feeling had gone completely and the room felt quite warm and normal. I went to the bathroom and washed. I changed my nightclothes and went back to bed.'

I sat open-mouthed trying to absorb what Jean had been saying. 'Why didn't you wake me?' I asked.

Jean said it would not have achieved anything.

'What the hell was going on? Why did Henry allow this to happen? He has said many times he would protect you. Did you ask him for an explanation?'

Jean said that she did ask Henry what it was all about. 'I returned to the bedroom feeling better but still very shaken from the ordeal. I lay still and composed myself. Henry's voice came through loud and clear. I could not see him but his voice had that familiar tone of confidence and authority that I have grown to respect and love. He said he was sorry that I had been

19

so frightened, but assured me that at all times he was in control and monitoring the situation. "You could have fooled me, Henry. I've never felt so frightened in my life," I answered. "Good," was the reply from Henry.'

Jean asked Henry who had been responsible for the occurrence and why it had happened. Henry replied that no single individual had been responsible, but that it was a combined energy of thought and power from the darker side of the spirit world. He explained that he and Jean's other friends had constantly warned her of the dangers of opening the mind without control to the spirit world. He was pleased that she had taken notice of his warnings and would pass them on to others. He was aware that Jean would soon be working as a medium more openly with the general public and thus meeting many more people. He then used that old cliché, 'Actions speak louder than words'.

Henry said that in the development group Jean had been trained to sit for rescue work, always under strict control and with the support of spirit friends and circle sitters on hand. Tonight Henry had opened the door to the lower planes without Jean's request or knowledge because he felt that she should experience the power that is present at all times, and understand how potent and frightening that power could be. He had been in control of what was happening and would have removed the influence in due course. He said he was delighted that Jean had remembered to call on him when she had felt in danger from spirit. Henry had promised Jean from the first stages of her development that he would always be in close attendance and would see that no harm came to her.

Henry felt that this dramatic experience would be more effective than any number of warnings given to her verbally. Jean agreed, saying it was something that she would never forget. She told Henry never to do anything like that again without prior warning. He said he felt it was unnecessary for Jean to have any further similar experiences, to which Jean replied, 'Thank God for that.'

I was angry after listening to this story, and said I felt that Henry had gone too far. Jean said that she too had been angry at first, but after listening to Henry's explanation she had accepted all that he said and the reason behind it. I said that she was far more understanding than I would have been, at which she smiled and said, 'Maybe that's why I'm a medium, Bob, and you're not.' I agreed.

The rest of our visit passed without incident. What we had looked upon as a short, well-deserved rest for Jean had turned into a demonstration of frightening proportions of the power that is present in the lower planes of spirit. From that moment Jean has never felt frightened or threatened by spirit, since Henry, as always, has kept his promise.

We are continually aware of the protection we receive from spirit friends, and we will always treat spirit with respect and reverence. It frightens us when we hear of people who play about with psychic forces, having experienced the power that is present. Jean and I are protected from this power; others are not.

I feel that it is important to emphasise this other dimension of the spirit world, not to deter involvement but to instil an attitude of respect. Communication from the spirit world is a wonderful and inspiring facet of life, but the darker side is seldom given the coverage it should be. Some mediums will not even accept its existence or discuss it. This is one of the first topics that Jean and I discuss with interested parties, for we feel that *all* aspects of mediumship should be openly discussed, not just the pleasant side. Many people, mediums included, may never have the experience of linking with the lower planes of the spirit world, but an understanding and awareness of its existence are vital should communication ever take place. The Boy Scouts' motto, 'Be prepared', is appropriate in all types of spirit work.

Spirit communication is not only what you may witness at a private sitting or public demonstration of clairvoyance; medium-ship is not solely to bring the love and messages from our loved ones in the spirit world. Once the door to the spirit world is opened anyone may choose to enter through it, including the frightened, lonely and unpleasant souls. Jean welcomes them all and treats them all with equal love and respect, for she has accepted that she is the channel for spirit without partiality or segregation.

I must stress that not all those who live in the lower planes are cruel and malevolent, as some examples of the various types of spirit friends we have spoken with and helped from the lower planes will demonstrate.

People who have no religious belief or conviction of life after death are totally unprepared for what happens to them after they die. We have spoken to many souls who did not know or could not accept that they had passed over. This may sound strange but it is absolutely true. If there has been no education or understanding of life after death, the spirit when released from the physical body becomes confused as it enters this strange new environment. The confusion is more common in the circumstances of a very sudden death.

Let us imagine that you are driving along in your car, happily listening to the radio. The next instant your car is struck by another vehicle. In a matter of seconds your spirit is projected from its earthly life, and your next conscious experience is that of your spirit *outside* the physical body. 'Where am I? What is happening?' These and many other questions flood into your consciousness. We have spoken to people who actually saw their physical remains being transported from the scene of the accident to the hospital. They could not understand what had happened. 'But that was me I saw being taken to hospital, and I'm here and all right. Why can't they see me? If I'm here and alive, who's that in the ambulance?' You see how confusing this situation must be to anyone who did not believe in life after death. We then have the very difficult task of trying to explain to them that their spirit has left the physical body, and the physical world, and they have 'died'. In many cases it takes a long time for us to get them to realise this. When we succeed, our friends who work with us from the spirit world take over the responsibility and accompany them on their first nervous steps in that world. Sometimes they are reunited with loved ones already there. These relatives and friends also help and comfort them on their voyage of discovery. We have heard from spirit friends how they attended their own funerals, still not accepting that they had died. Some have said that it was like a nightmare, and that Jean was simply a stranger talking to them as they dreamed. We have to be careful not to increase the fear or panic already there, and this demands great diplomacy in certain cases.

When on the other hand a person passes to spirit as the result of a long illness, there is usually a time of adjustment to the inevitable. The actual passing is often welcomed and the sufferer prepared for the spirit's transition. Even if the patient does not believe in life after death, the spiritual realisation of the truth is not so traumatic as in the case of a sudden or violent death. We feel privileged to have had the opportunity to speak to some people in these circumstances before they have died, and the communication Jean has received from them after their passing to the spirit world has been very moving. They have thanked us for helping them to accept the truth more quickly once it became apparent, rather than becoming confused and frightened. A common remark has been 'You were absolutely right, Jean, it's wonderful here. How could I have not believed in life after death? Thank you.'

When people pass to spirit without knowledge or understanding they can become trapped in their own ignorance and fear. One memorable example of this was a young boy who passed into the world of spirit alone and afraid.

We had chosen this particular evening in circle to devote to rescue work. Jean had asked Henry to allow friends from the lower planes to link with the group so that we might help them if we could. Joan was a nursing sister and a very good medium who had been sitting with our group for some years. Jean had expressed to Joan her feeling that she would never demonstrate

23

her mediumship on a public platform, that she was what we term a 'circle medium'. Joan had agreed with Jean's assessment and said that this was the type of involvement she wanted. Because of the nature of Joan's work in the hospital she was a magnet to those in spirit who needed our help.

Jean soon became aware of a young boy who had drawn close to Joan, and Joan agreed that she had felt his presence for some time. They both said they had the feeling that this was a very emotional case and warned the group to be prepared for what might follow. I asked Joan how she felt, and she said that she felt lonely and afraid. She became very quiet and we could sense that the little boy had taken Joan under deep control. Suddenly he began to scream and shout, 'I can't get out! Help me, help me, please somebody help me!' The screams were horrendous but eventually, after a long time, we were able to calm him down and get him to talk more rationally. He said he had been playing hide and seek on a rubbish site and had chosen to hide inside an old fridge. When he was inside the door had slammed shut and he had been unable to open it. You can imagine the fear and desperation this poor child suffered before eventually passing to spirit. He was still trapped in this small dark prison, still terrified and lost. Joan had opened her mind to the dark side of spirit and had reached out and touched our frightened young friend. We talked to him, explaining that he was no longer trapped in the fridge but was free and could now move wherever he chose. Through communication we discovered that he had owned a pet dog that had died some time before. We explained to him that if he thought of his pet and sent out loving thoughts to it they would be together again. We continued to talk to him, comforting and reassuring him that he was no longer in danger and was now safe with friends waiting to help him.

Joan slowly came back to normal consciousness, and when I had made sure that she was all right Lucy, Jean's spirit friend, came through to talk to us. She said that the little boy had found his dog and she would take them off together and reunite them with relatives and other friends. We could sense Lucy walking along holding this little boy's hand, his favourite dog in his other hand, as he went to meet his loved ones and other children.

One evening we were speaking to a man who had been killed in the war. He too had died alone and was trapped in the lower planes as a result of his religious belief. He said he had not received absolution before he died, so he felt he could not progress in the spirit world until this was granted. It was fortunate that Philip, a member of our group, had received training as a Catholic priest in his youth, so he was able to conduct a small service and give the man what he required. He then felt able to leave the dark side of the spirit world and commence his spiritual journey in his own true faith.

We can never always be certain of success in our work with those in the lower planes. One woman with whom we communicated demonstrated this fact when she told us of the circumstances of her passing to the spirit world. She had died in a German concentration camp. She knew exactly where she was and was happy to be in spirit away from the cruel and inhuman behaviour to which she and her family had been subjected. She said that her husband and children, who had also been killed in the camp, were with her. When I enquired how we could help her she asked me one of the most difficult questions I have ever been faced with. 'I saw my children and husband brutally humiliated and killed. I still feel vengeance and hatred towards those who carried out this act. I know I cannot progress spiritually until I can find forgiveness in my heart, but I have tried and found it impossible. Could you forgive those who killed your family in these circumstances?' I tried to imagine how I would have felt, and was unable to offer any assistance without a feeling of hypocrisy. I said that we would send our thoughts out to her and her family, asking that somehow she might discover a way to move away from her understandable attitude and find peace and happiness.

It is not only in circle that we have met inhabitants from the darker planes, but also when we have been asked to help people in their own homes. For this reason Jean always takes reliable friends with her to a house, unless she is absolutely sure that the problem is not the result of a malevolent spirit. Although she is protected by Henry, she may require the help of friends acquainted with this type of work to talk to the spirit as well and offer assistance.

One day a friend telephoned saying that she was very worried about a woman who had become suicidal and had been receiving professional help without much success. It had been suggested that the woman begin a course of tranquillisers and our friend was not at all happy with this. She explained that as far as she knew there was no obvious reason for the woman's state of mind. She felt it might be spirit influence and asked if we would assess the situation. We explained that we would need the permission of the woman and her family before we could offer our help, and were told this had been agreed. We said that we would come as quickly as possible.

On arriving we were told by the husband that a priest had performed a blessing on the house but that his wife's depression and suicidal tendencies had persisted. I was surprised that Jean did not request that she might walk round the house, as was her habit. She asked if anyone had been trying to communicate with spirit before our arrival. The man said a long time ago they had played with a Ouija board with some friends but they had had little success. Jean smiled and shook her head. 'You had more success than you thought,' she said. Then she asked if the children were all right and if anyone had felt anything unpleasant in the house. The husband looked rather confused but said that everything seemed normal except for his wife's unnatural depression and suicidal tendencies. We asked where his wife was and he said she was at a neighbour's house with the children. Jean asked if he would mind going round to the neighbour for a short while until we had finished doing what was necessary. The friend who had phoned was with us, and Jean said she could stay in his absence, since as we were strangers to the family he might understandably be concerned to leave us in his house. He said he didn't mind, and we promised to fetch him when we had finished our work.

Besides the friend of the family and Jean and myself, there were four other circle members with us. When the husband left Jean said she had seen a man standing in the corner of the room laughing at us. She knew that he was a very disturbed soul on account of his behaviour and cynical attitude. I could now understand why Jean had not wished to walk round the house and had asked the husband to leave. She told us to prepare for a very difficult rescue.

Jean put herself in a receptive state and soon we were able to make some kind of communication. We soon realised that we would have difficulty in getting through to this man in these circumstances. I suggested to Muriel and Bill, two of our close friends in the circle, that I would like to try something we had never tried before – to persuade the man to accompany us back to our house. This would involve Muriel and Bill and me constantly talking to him, while Jean, we hoped, would keep the link with him during the short journey home. I explained my intention to the others and they helped Jean into the car, and the communication continued until she was seated in her usual chair in our sitting room. Meanwhile the friend explained briefly to the family that we had had to leave but that we would return and hopefully explain what had happened.

Our home has been used for spirit communication for twenty years, during which time an atmosphere has been built that obviously helps with communication. I felt that if we could bring our friend into a more spiritually energised environment it would help us in getting through to him. He was a very angry spirit. Because of the treatment he had received from other people he had committed suicide, and he was determined to seek revenge at the first opportunity that was offered to him. This came about when the husband and wife had played with the Ouija board. Because the wife was the weakest personality present the spirit had turned his influence on her. It had taken a long time, but eventually he was succeeding in his revenge by influencing another to do as he had done – namely, commit suicide.

It became apparent that he had always been a strong atheist and had no religious belief whatsoever. When the vicar had come to bless the house our friend told us that he had laughed at the ritual and the symbolic use of the cross and holy water. It was useless to try to persuade him by means of any religious philosophy. We could only use common sense and attempt to show him that by influencing another person to follow his actions he would achieve absolutely nothing. We explained that the woman would now be protected and that he could not hurt her at all. We told him that in using his revenge to try to hurt others he would invoke a much stronger power that would eventually turn its influence on himself. During the whole communication he had used obscenities and foul language to try to frighten and intimidate us, all to no avail. The rescue ended with the sitting-room door being slammed shut. It startled us all but his presence had gone.

We returned to the house and explained in simple terms that the wife had been under the influence of spirit. We explained that she was now protected by our spirit friends and that she would soon return to the normal person they knew and loved. We kept a close eye on the situation through the friend of the family and were pleased to hear that after a short time the wife did indeed return to her normal self. The couple promised that they would never again try any form of spirit communication.

For us this particular case was not a wholly successful rescue since we were unable to help a disturbed soul on his spiritual path, but we felt some satisfaction in breaking the hold he had over a woman who was unable to help herself. This dramatic example proves that our warnings against dabbling with spirit are not just a ploy: *the danger does exist*.

Ray was a very good friend of Jean's and mine and had sat in circle with us for some time. His wife Marian had previously been invited to join our group and had shown signs of being

what we call an 'automatic writer' for spirit. This is the phenomenon of spirits controlling the hand of a sitter and writing
their message on paper. The sitter has no control over what is
being written; spirit simply uses the sitter's hand and the pen.
Marian had said that she would suddenly feel the compulsion
to write, and then spirit would take control of her hand and
write down what it wished to say.

Marian explained that Ray did not believe in any form of
spirit communication and had been very reluctant to let her
attend. We said that he would be welcome to come along as a
spectator, provided that he did not disrupt the proceedings.
After attending for some months Ray began to show a distinct
interest in what was taking place, and asked if he might be
allowed to join in the group's activities. He did not want to
train as a medium, for it was obvious that he had no such
ability, but he said that when Henry or Lucy or our other
friends were communicating he had so many questions he
would like to ask and would be very interested in their answers.
So we agreed, and in the year or so that Ray attended he became
totally convinced of the fact of life after death. His scepticism
was completely removed.

Some years later a tragic event took place which completely
shattered Jean, myself and the members of the group with whom
Ray had been involved. We had not kept close contact with
Marian and Ray since they had left the group. They were both
working full-time, and their priority was their family not spirit.
This is an attitude that Jean and I endorse, and we always tell
new sitters that their family must come first. When the time is
right and they wish to continue their spirit work we will do
what we can to help them.

Marian had sent us a few examples of the 'writing' that she
had received, but naturally the frequency of this form of
communication had lessened after they left the group. We were
pleasantly surprised to have an unexpected visit from Marian
one day. She was very upset and worried about Ray, however.
He had been suffering from severe stomach pains and his doctor

had referred him to a specialist for further tests. Ray was convinced that he had cancer and had cancelled many appointments at the hospital because he dreaded his fears being confirmed. Marian asked Jean if it was possible for her friends in spirit to give Ray a true diagnosis of his problem. Jean said she would ask Henry and Lucy and pass on their answer. The message was that Ray had merely got a twisted gut and that an operation would easily clear up the problem. On hearing this Ray promised that he would make his appointment at the hospital.

You can imagine how devastated we were when Marian rang to say that Ray had hanged himself. On the day of his appointment Marian had offered to drive with him to the hospital. Ray had said that he would prefer to go alone, so Marian had reluctantly agreed and gone to work. Once there she felt the compulsion to return home, and it was then that she discovered Ray's body.

We felt the same guilt as everyone in not having made sure that Ray had accepted spirit's diagnosis and that his mind had been restored to a more rational state. But it is always easy to see one's own faults after the event. The whole group attended the funeral, and Marian asked us if we would return to the house to make sure that Ray was not trapped there as a result of his action. This was not the case, and we talked to Marian at great length to convince her that there was nothing she should feel guilty about. No one had appreciated just how strongly Ray had been affected by his problem. We explained that we felt that his involvement in our group had been for a reason none of us could understand at the time. We knew that, even though his passing to spirit had been tragic and self-induced, he was now at peace and would understand the truth of life after death. We felt that we had been part of a rescue operation, only in Ray's case it had taken place before his transition to the spirit world.

The post-mortem confirmed Jean's message from spirit: Ray had been suffering from a twisted intestine and there was no sign at all of cancer. This only made the whole affair more sickening and gave us the feeling of a life having been wasted, but we are not in a position to judge or pass opinions on such an event. It happened, and maybe in the future we will have a clearer understanding. Until then we miss the physical contact of a good friend.

We were delighted to hear recently that Marian has now remarried and is living in the same house with her new husband Len. She has said that she would be pleased for me to include Ray's story in this book. I know that Ray would not object, as he received tremendous help from spirit both before and after his passing. Marian and Len are very happy and do not feel it necessary to move house. Ray is continuing on his pathway in the spirit world and we know he would be pleased for Marian that she has found another partner.

You will see from these few examples that the lower planes of spirit are not only inhabited by the unpleasant types of spirit but also by the lost and frightened, and to these it is possible to offer help and guidance through the gift of mediumship. I applaud the dedication and sacrifice shown by all mediums involved in this aspect of mediumship, and admire them for using their gift to help those in spirit who need helping.

Jean is often approached after a sitting or a public demonstration and told how wonderful it must be to receive all the messages of love and guidance from the loved ones in the spirit world. Many people have said how they envy her ability, and that she must feel like a star standing on the platform. Jean always replies that they should see any medium just before he or she steps out on to that platform. She mentions the years of hard, dedicated work that have led to her public demonstrations, and emphasises that mediumship is not all 'love and roses' and that what they have just seen is only a small part of her work, the nice part. 'It would probably scare the pants off you if you only knew the truth,' she adds.

Next time you see a medium giving a public demonstration please try to remember that the medium may have had a similar experience to Jean. Give a thought to Jean in that small room in London, alone and afraid and feeling she was about to die. The life of a medium is not a glamorous life. It is hard work and not always pleasant, but it does bring its own rewards. I know Jean would never choose any other life, and nor would I.

Chapter Three

Helping the Police

It was Monday, 10 March 1975. We had been sitting in the home circle for only a few minutes when Jean became aware of a young girl from spirit who had drawn close to her. Jean told the group that she could feel a sensation of choking and strangulation. She said she was in a dark and frightening place: she could hear water flowing from somewhere beneath her. She was standing on a small ledge and there was a steel ladder leading down some sort of shaft. She then said that bags of some kind were tied to her bound legs; she described them as sandbags or something similar. Her hands were also bound together.

Jean felt terrified. Then she became aware of a man climbing down the ladder from a manhole cover or a kind of lid. She gave the following description of the man: he was about five feet seven inches tall, of slim build and with dark hair; he had a signet ring on a finger of his right hand and square fingernails that were dirty. He had a northern accent and Jean could hear the name Donald. Then she saw a girl hanging from a wire or rope with something hanging from her feet. She said, 'My name is Leslie. Tell them I'll be with them at Mary's.'

At the beginning of the year a young girl, the daughter of a wealthy family from Highley, a small town about ten miles from where we live, had been kidnapped. The Whittles were a well-known business family involved in coach and bus hire. Their daughter Leslie had been taken from her home and a nationwide search and investigation had been launched by the West Midlands police force. Leslie's body was eventually found in an underground culvert at Kidsgrove near Stoke-on-Trent. She had been tied hand and foot and pushed off a ledge half-way down the entrance shaft to the underground storm-water culvert.

On 14 March, Leslie's funeral was held at St Mary's Church in Highley.

The man responsible was still at large, and the police were asking anyone who had any information at all to contact them. On Sunday, 27 April, Jean and I with Muriel and Bill went to the police headquarters at Kidderminster police station and told them all the information Jean had received from spirit in our own home circle.

A few days later two men came to the house. They said they were detectives from Kidderminster and would like to discuss the information we had given on the Sunday. There had obviously been a lot of media coverage on the discovery of Leslie's body and details of how she had died. The detectives were very curious about what we had said, as Jean had mentioned exact details of the culvert and how Leslie had been killed that had never been published. They said that only the police, Leslie and the murderer himself could know the intimate details we had supplied. The looks that the detectives were giving me made me feel very uncomfortable, and I felt sure that they suspected me. From their questioning of Jean it was obvious that they were seeking proof of her ability as a medium. Thank goodness Jean and spirit came through.

We were sitting drinking coffee when Jean suddenly spoke to one of the detectives. 'Your mother's in spirit and she is talking to me. Your name is Brian and your wife is Mary.' Jean then began to describe the detective's mother and how she had passed. She talked about the holiday that was cancelled and

34

how they would shortly be moving house, and that the house was not their first choice for there had been some disappointment.

The detective sat open-mouthed as Jean carried on giving him evidence of other friends in the spirit world who were related to him. His name was indeed Brian and his wife was Mary. They had hoped to have an early holiday but owing to the murder enquiries all holidays had been cancelled. They had been outbid for the house they originally wanted and the house they were soon moving to was their second choice. He said all the other details Jean gave were absolutely true. We then spent about an hour talking about mediumship and our work for spirit. As the detectives were leaving, Brian said that, should we receive any further information regarding the case, would we please pass it on to the police.

Some time later a man similar to the person Jean had described was arrested and convicted of the murder. His name was Donald Neilson.

There have been other occasions when the police have asked Jean for assistance, especially in the case of missing people. By holding an object belonging to a missing person Jean can use her gift of psychometry to provide information that has been very useful. We have been asked not to disclose any details of these events, and to keep Jean's credibility and integrity I have no intention of breaking that trust.

One case, however, was not directly linked with the police, although the person concerned told the police that she was coming to see Jean for a private sitting. The police said they would be very interested in what Jean might have to say.

The woman told Jean that she didn't want evidence of life after death but she had heard that Jean might be able to help in offering information about her missing sister. She had brought a piece of jewellery that her sister had often worn before she disappeared in strange circumstances. Jean at that point knew nothing of the events surrounding the disappearance, and she gave the following message. 'First of all your sister is still alive. I get a feeling of guilt, and that she is afraid to come home for some reason. I can sense the presence of a man but he is no longer with her. She is somewhere south; I get the feeling of Bristol or somewhere in that area. I can feel steam and heat, lots of steam. I feel I'm in a launderette or a chip-shop, somewhere with a lot of steam and people. I feel that your sister will come back in due course, but only when she feels she can face the family. I don't know why I feel this guilt. Maybe you can answer this?'

The woman replied that her sister had gone off with her husband but the husband had returned some time later alone. The police had been informed and the husband had been suspected of ill-treating the sister and had been questioned intensively. He had denied all charges.

Following Jean's feelings from the piece of jewellery, we heard from the family that enquiries were made in the area, and from a photograph that was shown it was learnt that for a short time she had indeed worked as an assistant in a launderette in Bristol. She had left and no further knowledge of her whereabouts was to be found. Jean reaffirmed her feeling that at some time in the future she would contact the family and return home. We have not heard whether this has yet happened, but Jean is confident that it will.

On another occasion a woman came to see Jean for a private sitting, very upset about losing her dogs. During the sitting Jean suddenly exclaimed that the dogs were not dead, but had been stolen. The woman confessed that she had not told Jean that the dogs had been stolen to see whether, when she said that she had lost her dogs, Jean would automatically give her some evidence that they were 'happy and safe' in spirit. Jean wagged her finger at the woman, admonishing her for trying to trick her. She said that although the dogs had been stolen she could not get any other information that might be of help. The woman thanked Jean and apologised for not being totally open about the circumstances. Apparently she had been returning from Cruft's after showing her pedigree dogs and while she had left the van unattended thieves had forced the doors and made off with them.

Another experience Jean had was linked to a tragic case that received mass publicity: the death of Maria Caldwell, the little girl who was beaten and abused by her father and died in awful circumstances. On Monday, 10 February 1975 a little girl drew near to Jean in our home circle. The child was very frightened and Jean felt that she was crouching in a broom cupboard or some tiny confined space. We had great difficulty in getting her to talk to us. Over the next few weeks we gradually gained her confidence enough for her to say that her name was Maria. We had all felt that it was Maria Caldwell who was communicating, but she was so afraid and said so little that we could not be sure. With the help of our spirit friends we were able to convince her that she was no longer in danger from anyone and she was eventually persuaded to go along with Lucy and join other spirit children.

As the child was leaving for the last time we were given what we feel was proof that it was indeed Maria. She said to Jean, 'Please take care of Teddy for me, he will need your help.' We all assumed that she was referring to her own teddy bear, or maybe a pet of some kind. A week later it was reported in the national papers that another little boy had been beaten to death by his father in the same area where Maria had lived. His Christian name was Edward.

These few examples of the variety of ways in which Jean's gift is used demonstrate that a medium's life is not all roses. The police do seek the assistance of mediums and psychics, and at times they receive very useful information. Understandably perhaps, they prefer not to make this fact public knowledge, and we accept their reasons for this, but in one way it is sad. For if more people knew that mediumship can be used in a constructive way within the community, it might help to improve the image of mediums.

Chapter Four

Happy Haunting

The telephone rang and a woman's voice said that we would not know her but that she had been to our public meetings and had been impressed by what she had seen. She had passed our names on to a friend who would be getting in touch with us very soon. I thanked her for her recommendation and asked if her friend would be asking for a private sitting. The woman said she couldn't give us any details other than the name of her friend who would be ringing very soon. I was rather puzzled by the secrecy until I received the call, when the reason became obvious.

The next morning the woman whose name we had been given telephoned. She spoke in a very authoritative voice, asking if she was speaking to a Mr Robert Cull? I replied that indeed she was and that her friend had told us to expect her call. She explained that she was the private secretary to a family whose name we would know immediately. She then told me the name of the family. I almost dropped the telephone when she told me, and asked what on earth she needed to phone us for.

The woman explained that the family had some problems at their home and were having difficulty keeping the staff. The housekeeper and the rest of the staff could not stay in one of the rooms owing to the phenomena that took place there. She said that the family had instructed her to find someone reliable to clear up this problem as soon as possible. The family were in America and would be returning home for the Christmas holidays. There would be many guests and relatives staying over Christmas and they wanted no unpleasant incidents during that time.

The secretary said that enquiries had been made by herself and the directors of the family business and we had been highly recommended for this type of work. I said that Jean and myself had helped many people in similar circumstances, and we felt privileged to be invited to offer our services in this particular case. The secretary said that the family had been informed and had agreed to our visiting the house provided that under no circumstances should any publicity whatsoever be given before, during or after the event. This had been stressed very strongly by the family, and serious consequences might ensue should this trust ever be broken. I explained that Jean and I always took our work seriously and that we ourselves would not accept the invitation if we thought the media would be present on our visit. The secretary said this was one of the reasons we had been selected. I said that we did not want to know any details about the kind of problem they were experiencing, for if Jean could help them to overcome it her lack of knowledge about the circumstances would be more convincing for all concerned.

Our promise of secrecy to the family still stands, so all I can say about them is that they are very well known and have business outlets and connections all over the world. The house we were invited to was their home in Great Britain.

It was early in December 1985 that we set off to drive to the house. We had allowed plenty of time, for it was a long way to drive. Jean said very little as we drove there except that she was pleased the family would not be at home as it would have made her more nervous than she was already. We arrived in the village near the house with about an hour to spare. We went into a hotel in the village and asked for coffee in the lounge. The waiter asked if we were visiting anyone in the area, and we replied that we were 'just passing through'.

We followed the directions we had been given and eventually came to a private lane leading up to the house. The large entrance gates were open and a notice stated the family name and gave a very clear warning to trespassers. As we passed through the gates Jean said, 'Oh well, here we go. Come on, Henry, please don't let me down; and, Lucy, you stay very close to me too.' I smiled to myself, thinking how Lucy would be reacting to the situation, and told Jean that she must be saying in her lovely cockney accent, 'Gaw blimey, this is a bit posh, ain't it? I'd berra be'ave meself or they'll throw me out of 'ere.' We were both laughing when we found the side-door and parked the car, for I didn't think my old Maxi would look quite right somehow if I had parked it outside the front entrance.

We rang the bell and the door was opened by a young woman. 'Mr and Mrs Cull? We have been expecting you. Please come in.' She introduced herself as Mary, the housekeeper, and led us into a lovely room off the kitchen, with a log fire burning and a large old scrubbed table in the centre. She asked if we would like some coffee and we said that would be nice. We wondered where the private secretary was, as she had said she would be there when we arrived. Mary came back with a pot of coffee and told us that the secretary had rung before we arrived to say she had been held up with a business meeting but would be arriving shortly.

When we had finished the coffee Jean moved over to a very old wooden rocking-chair that was near to the fire. It was a very cold day, and the warmth of the log fire was like a magnet. Jean sat with her eyes closed, rocking slowly to and fro, and I noticed she had that particular smile that told me she was talking to spirit. After a few minutes she opened her eyes and looked past me towards the door. 'You have been talking to someone, haven't you, and you can see someone as well,' I said. Jean smiled and nodded. I gave a sigh of relief; at least Jean was aware of spirit in the house.

Shortly afterwards Margaret, the private secretary, arrived and introduced herself. She said she didn't know what was involved in this situation, and asked if there was anything Jean required to help her with her work. Jean said the only thing she would like was permission to walk round the house by herself. She explained that if she was on her own there would be no distractions and she could use her senses more acutely. In this way she hoped to be able to identify the room where the problem was occurring and find out who might be responsible. Margaret said that Jean had total freedom to go wherever she liked, and if she got lost she should simply push one of the many bells round the house and they would show which room she was in. Jean smiled and said she wouldn't get lost. 'You forget, I will not be walking around on my own.' We laughed and Jean left the room.

Mary came back with fresh coffee for Margaret and the three of us sat discussing what might take place. They were both very interested and showed obvious relief when I explained that nothing weird or strange would happen. After about twenty minutes Jean returned to the parlour. Mary and Margaret looked at Jean with some apprehension. Jean must have sensed their anxiety, for she said, 'What a lovely home. There is a lovely friendly atmosphere in the house. There has been much love and happiness expressed here, except for two rooms.'

'*Two* rooms?' Mary answered with surprise. 'I thought there was only one room that had the presence?'

Jean suggested that we all walk round the house together. After we had looked at several of the rooms she led us along a beautiful panelled corridor that led to a large room with double doors. She opened the doors and we went into a magnificent drawing room. As I stood admiring the décor and furniture I suddenly became aware of a different feeling in this room: it felt sad. I said nothing, however, waiting for the expert to speak. 'As soon as I walked into this room I was overcome with a very strong feeling of sadness.' I felt quite pleased with myself but said nothing, and Jean carried on. 'Nothing nasty has

41

happened in the room, but it seems strange for such a beautiful room to have this sad feeling. I also feel that the room is, or was, very special to someone.'

Mary said that she also felt sad when she came into the room, but that was because she knew what had happened there. Margaret then told us the story of a tragic death in the family some years ago. She admitted that everyone was concerned that it might be this person who was 'haunting' the house. Jean assured them that at no time had she been aware of this person in the house, although obviously her charisma or aura was still around the house as she was a senior member of the family and her influence in the house must have been very positive.

Margaret said that the person concerned had personally taken responsibility for the complete renovation and alteration of this room. She had added the conservatory that was adjacent and the doors leading into it from the room. When the renovation was completed she used the room as a private retreat and study, and did most of her business from this room. But she had died only weeks after the room was finished. Jean said that that was obviously the reason why she had sensed sadness. She added that the feelings were definitely not the result of the person returning with sadness in her heart, but of people like Mary coming into the room regularly and feeling sad about the circumstances.

Jean then led the way directly up two flights of stairs to a landing on the second floor. She walked along the passage and stopped by a door at the end. 'This is the room I'm more interested in.' I looked at Mary and Margaret, and their expressions told me that Jean had found the room that was causing the problem. Jean opened the door and walked in. The two women seemed reluctant to enter so I walked past them and went into the room. The atmosphere hit me as if a bucket of cold water had been thrown in my face – it was so positive that I gasped for breath. I stepped back out immediately and turned to Mary. 'Wow!' was all I could think of saying. Knowing what to expect, I now went slowly through the door. It was like walking through a curtain from a normal temperature into a deep-freeze. Jean was standing in the centre of the room. 'It's marvellous, isn't it? What an atmosphere.' She eventually persuaded Mary and Margaret to come into the room as well.

The room was very sparsely furnished, with a table and chairs and a few easy chairs scattered about. It was a good-sized room with a small door at the far end. Jean reassured Margaret and Mary that there was nothing at all to be frightened of. She said that spirit was very definitely present, but that it was not in any way malevolent. Then she smiled and said, 'Welcome to Edward's room!'

Mary and Margaret looked at each other with a puzzled look on their faces. 'Edward? Edward who?'

Jean said that Edward hadn't told her his surname; he was just Edward.

Mary said, 'You've spoken to him? But we haven't seen you talking to anyone while you've been here.'

Jean said that she had first met Edward when she was sitting by the fire in the parlour. She thought that he would be about five or six years old.

'You mean it's only a little boy?' Mary said, with a hint of guilt in her voice.

'That's right,' Jean replied. 'I feel this used to be his room at some time, and he says he likes playing with the children, especially with the trains. Do children often play in this room?'

Mary and Margaret were amazed. They said that it was the grandchildren's playroom, and that whenever the family got together the children always made a bee-line for this room. Mary went to the little door and from a bunch of keys on her hip took a key and opened the door into a large cupboard packed full of toys and games. Mary said it was interesting that Jean had mentioned trains. She rummaged through the toys and then gave me a beautiful toy train engine that was very old and still had the key in it to wind it up. She said that the children claimed to have found it one day in the room, and the family swore that it had never been bought as the train sets were all electric. The room had been completely bare when it was first turned into a playroom. Jean said she felt it was one of Edward's toys that he had 'apported', or brought back, for his friends to play with. Jean asked Mary what had she experienced in the room that had frightened her so much.

Mary said that every time she came into the room to clean up after the children she could feel the presence of someone watching her. Jean said that that was understandable. Mary said that often when she bent down to pick up a toy or something off the floor she had felt breath on the side of her face. She had also felt a definite tug on her skirt many times. Mary said that what had frightened her most of all was the vacuum cleaner being switched on and off all the time she was in the room. She said sometimes it happened so often that she would pack up the vacuum and run out of the room, slamming the door behind her. She said she became so afraid that she only ever went into the room if it was absolutely necessary.

'Oh, what a shame,' Jean said, 'he was just trying to get you to notice him. He probably played with the vacuum because he had never seen one before and enjoyed switching it on and off.' Jean said she felt that Edward had died of either whooping cough or bronchitis, for he had a very nasty cough. Obviously he hadn't got the cough now, but he had just shown it to her as evidence. She said that she was sure she could persuade Edward to leave if that was what the family and Mary really wanted.

Jean then asked if they knew a tall, very upright gentleman dressed in military uniform, who she had the feeling was in the Guards. Margaret said she would go to the kitchen and ask Cook to come and join them. Mary explained that Cook had lived in the village all her life and might know something about the previous owners. Cook arrived with Margaret, and Jean described both Edward and the man whom she thought was Edward's father. Cook said that the family who had lived in the house many years ago did lose a young son, and they moved out shortly after his death. Cook said that she was only a girl at the time but she could remember a man as Jean had described him, and that although she couldn't remember the name he was definitely a Colonel something or other.

Jean said she felt that Edward's father had come along to take him away if he was causing a nuisance. Mary said that if it was possible she would like Jean to ask Edward to stay, for now that she knew who he was it was a shame to send him off. Mary said that what had frightened her more than anything was not knowing who or what the presence was. Jean said that in future when Mary came into the room she should speak to Edward, saying things like, 'Hello, Edward, it's only me coming to clean up the room again. Don't play with the vacuum as it takes me longer to finish,' and so on. Mary said that it was uncanny, for she had heard someone coughing on the stairs leading from the room and she could have sworn she heard footsteps following her down the stairs. When Jean was satisfied that no one else was around and that Mary and Margaret were happy and had no more questions, she said that she had finished. Cook invited us to have some scones and biscuits she had made.

As we sat talking in the kitchen about similar experiences we had been asked to help with, Cook said she had never believed in such 'stuff and nonsense' until now. She knew Jean could not possibly have known before about the room or the children, and she liked the way Jean treated spirit, without all that seance nonsense. After more discussion over our home-made tea we said we would have to leave as we had a long drive home. Jean said they must let us know if they wanted Edward out of the house, but it was not necessary for us to return because Lucy had now made the link with Edward, and would take care of him at any time.

We have not heard from the family since, so we can only assume that everyone is happy sharing their lovely home with a previous occupier.

There have been other occasions when we were called to a

45

house to help the inhabitants who said they were being troubled by spirit, only to find that spirit was quite happy in that situation and did not need or want our help. In these circumstances we simply identified who the spirit was, which usually defused the situation and brought peace of mind to those living in the house. They often asked us not to 'remove' their 'ghost' and then lived happily together.

A man from Wolverhampton called us to say that his daughter had for a long time described someone dressed in a long black cloak who walked round the house. The man said that the family was not afraid of the spirit and nothing frightening had taken place. They were simply curious as to who it was who was sharing their home.

When we were certain that it was not a malevolent presence we decided that we would go and see them, taking with us the development group we were training at the time. We thought it would be a good opportunity for them to put into practice what they were being trained for. We got the agreement of the family, who were pleased to oblige, and asked if a few other members of the family could also be present as they were fascinated by the whole subject. I said we would not object provided that everyone adopted a serious attitude and did not treat the occasion as a party. I made it quite clear that we would be there solely to help spirit, and to make sure spirit was not in distress or in need of help. We explained to the members of the group what we expected from them, and passed on all the information we had been given, which was very little – namely a person in a long black cloak. Jean said she would use her own sensitivity but would keep her findings to herself.

When we arrived the family plus three other relatives were waiting. Our group including Jean and myself totalled seven. I asked the family not to give us any further information, and Jean then went to the daughter's bedroom by herself. The rest of the group passed the time in conversation with the family until Jean returned. Jean nodded to me, and I asked the group to go together and come back to the room when they chose.

We finally congregated in the sitting room to discuss the findings.

During the absence of the group Jean had told the family that she had seen and spoken to a lady who was dressed in an old-fashioned long shawl. Jean felt this was what the daughter had mistaken for a long black cloak. She also mentioned that she had been aware of a lot of spirit children in the house. When the group returned to the room they looked a little nervous as Jean and I sat waiting to hear their assessment. They knew from past experience how strict Jean was and how seriously she took her work for spirit.

All of the group had been aware of a spirit presence. They said that the person the daughter had probably seen was an old lady dressed in a long old-fashioned shawl, and that they had all been aware of a lot of children in the house. Then they sat in silence looking at Jean. I smiled to myself, sensing their feelings as they waited for Jean's reaction. The family broke the tension by saying they had repeated word for word what Jean had seen and sensed. There were smiles all round and I was aware of the feeling of achievement coming from the group. Jean smiled and looked pleased too, but then became more serious again. 'Well done, but we haven't finished yet. We agree on who is present, but there are a lot of questions still to be answered. Has anyone heard a name? Does the lady need our help? Why have we got the children? Why here in this house? Come on now, let's get some answers.'

The group asked if they could return to the bedroom and sit with Jean while they tried to communicate with the lady. I stayed talking to the family as they all returned to the bedroom. Eventually, following the group's communications with the old lady, this information was given to the family.

Jean had begun by asking the family if there was anyone they knew who had lived in the street during the war. The father said there was an old lady a few doors away who had lived in the street all her life. Jean said that was good, as she might be able to confirm some of the information they had received. The old lady Jean had communicated with had said her name was Emily. She had died in the house and was a spinster. During the war she had taken care of many children while their parents were at work. She had been regarded as the 'granny' of the street. She said the children used to come and visit her, for they knew they would always get cake or treats of some sort. Emily was obviously still doing her granny job, but now it was with spirit children. She certainly did not need any help from us, and was very happy loving and caring for the children. She must have enjoyed her house and her role as the adopted gran, and was simply continuing her wonderful work still in her own home. We said to the family how marvellous to know that their house was the haven for spirit children in need of the love of a granny.

We heard later that the lady still living in the street remembered Emily very well, and had confirmed that we had exactly described her character and loving nature, especially towards children. The houses have been demolished since our meeting with Emily, but we know that she is still carrying on her work looking after spirit children. God bless her: we often send our prayers and thoughts to her.

It is important to learn from these two stories that you should never jump to conclusions should you feel you have a spirit presence in your home. Don't assume that the spirit must be malevolent, or that it is there to hurt or frighten you. In some cases spirit may simply be continuing their spirit life, totally oblivious of your presence. If they begin to move objects, make noises or do any of the numerous things spirit do to make their presence known, it is usually because they need help in some way. Because they cannot communicate with you, they will disturb your normal way of life until you seek the help of someone who *can* communicate.

If the presence does not offend or frighten you, then just enjoy the privilege of sharing your house with your spirit friends. I can promise you they will not harm you. I speak from years of personal experience in sharing our home with numerous spirit friends. We feel honoured that they should choose us as their friends. Jean and I have often said that our home would feel very empty and lonely without them.

Chapter Five

Spiritual Help

Since their advent in 1848, what we refer to as modern-day spiritualism and mediumship have changed dramatically with the passage of time. The very slow and laborious methods of communication with spirit have greatly improved and been perfected by the co-operation of spirit and mediums. When you think that communication was first achieved by tilting a table in response to questions asked of spirit, or tapping a series of raps to correspond to letters of the alphabet, you will see how primitive and long-winded a process it was. If spirit were still using this form of communication, Jean would need to space her sittings many hours apart rather than the hour that now separates them.

The image of a medium sitting opposite the sitter round a table in a darkened room and then going into a form of trance while 'the voices' speak has long gone. The attitude towards spirit guides (our spirit friends) has at last become more sensible among the majority of genuine mediums. The ridiculous myth that all mediums have a Red Indian helping them has been dispelled. Mediums today like Jean realise and accept that their role has changed from that of a simple channel for spirit to pass on messages from the spirit world; they now act as counsellors and advisers, while still accepting that their prime responsibility is to prove the continuation of life after death.

The development classes of today, although conducted with the purpose of training novice mediums, are more inclined to be classes for the development of many other spiritual and mental faculties. The objective we have adopted in our own development classes over the years has been twofold. Obviously if people have mediumistic ability we encourage and develop their gift to the very best of their and our ability. More generally, however, we set out to heighten and increase the sensitivity of all members, so that they can use this new awareness in their everyday lives. Included in our programme for a new group is education and enlightenment on spirit and the spirit world. As we become more aware of the capabilities of our own minds, we automatically become more aware of our own spirituality. Hence there is a natural spiritual progression taking place hand in hand with a steady increase in sensitivity.

If you are ever invited to join a development class and find yourself sitting round a table in a dark room holding hands with the other members waiting for 'the spirits' to talk, leave as quickly as possible, for you are in the company of some very strange people.

We have found that spirit communication and the various methods spirit use for this phenomenon have changed according to the needs and attitudes of people from the early days. In my opinion two major events have influenced spirit communication more than any other, both as the result of a current need.

At the time of the two great wars, spirit were aware that millions of people would pass to the spirit world as the result of the senseless killing associated with war. Spirit knew that there would be a great demand by the relatives and friends left behind for evidence and proof that their loved ones had not been taken from them for ever. They needed to know that loved ones killed in the wars were at peace; those who had no body to bury or pay their last respects to needed comfort and reassurance. Mediumship and spiritualism during this period attracted vast audiences at meeting halls and churches. The demonstration of 'physical' mediumship was at a premium. It is also a sad fact that many charlatan mediums were very much in the public eye at that time.

The reason for the popularity of physical mediums can be attributed to two unique circumstances. The first is the great number of people who needed absolute proof of life after death. Physical mediumship proves this beyond doubt, as it requires no mental co-operation between the sitter and the medium. The evidence of the presence of spirit is achieved by purely physical means. The people witnessing physical phenomena by spirit need only their physical senses to become aware of spirit's presence. Communication from spirit had to be easily recognised and understood. Spirit responded to this need, hence the greater number of physical mediums.

The second reason for more physical mediums at that time than today was the general lifestyle. There was no television, and even the radio was considered a luxury. The pace of life was much slower, and people had more time to make their own entertainment. Mediums could find people willing to sit with them for the years of slow development required for their physical mediumship. It was not uncommon for a physical medium to spend as long as fifteen to twenty years in developing this amazing method of spirit communication. I believe this is the main reason that there are so few physical mediums practising today. Living as we do in an instant world, we wouldn't have the patience to spend this length of time developing our gift.

The second major event that has changed the method of spirit communication is the advance of technology in the second half of the twentieth century. With this we have moved from a simple lifestyle to a highly sophisticated one. Our spiritual values diminished, to be replaced by a greedy materialistic attitude. When consumer products became more easily available we couldn't get enough. We became obsessed with acquiring as many possessions as we could (or could not) afford.

Spirit became very concerned about the retreat from religion that was taking place. People's priorities moved from religious conviction and spiritual attainment to purely material wealth. With the introduction of more effective means of communication, spirit knew that a quicker and more refined method of proving their existence was also required. This is why there are so many more clairvoyant mediums today than ever before. The interest in the human mind is such that mental mediumship is now far more acceptable than it would have been in the early years of this century.

The dramatic increase in the number of people currently showing interest in the subject proves yet again that spirit have responded in the right manner at exactly the right time. The most common demonstrations of mediumship now concentrate less on the dramatic physical phenomena and more on the mental faculty of clairvoyance and clairaudience. I do feel, however, that a change is soon to be seen in a move back to more physical mediumship. Science is now taking a very great interest in mediumship and other extensions of the human mind. There are courses in what is termed 'parapsychology' in many universities. Because science needs to see *physical* evidence of mediumship, I am confident that spirit will respond and we will begin to see more development groups concentrating on physical mediumship.

Many of our healers are now accepting invitations from study groups investigating the physical changes taking place in patients following spiritual healing. Because of this obvious physical change, which can be seen and monitored by scientists, more and more spiritual healers are now accepted and allowed to work in conjunction with orthodox medical practitioners. Some people will always stick to the attitude that 'seeing is believing', which is difficult to overcome with mental mediumship.

Spirit are always aware of the needs of people still living this earthly life. They adapt their influence and guidance accordingly. As one of spirit's instruments Jean will be constantly changing her role as the inspiration and help from her spirit friends alter to suit the various needs of those who come to seek her help. But her main role as a medium proving that there is life after death will never change; that is spirit's most important priority. No matter how much life changes on earth, we will always want to know more about what may happen to us when we die. This thirst for knowledge of the unknown will remain with mankind for ever. Eventually everyone will know the truth about life after death: at the moment Jean is just a small spoke in a very large wheel of progress.

We were given dramatic proof of the spiritual importance of Jean's work very recently. A young woman came for a sitting and her grandmother, who was now in the spirit world, told her that she was taking care of the baby she had lost the year before. Then Jean said that her grandmother had just told her that Carolle was pregnant again. Carolle said yes, only that week she had had the pregnancy confirmed. Jean was puzzled by what the grandmother said next. 'I only took care of the baby in spirit till now. I gave her back to her mother, and this time she will be fine.'

Very cautiously Jean interpreted what she felt the grandmother was trying to say. 'I honestly believe that the baby you are carrying now has the same spirit that was intended for your first child. Was your first baby a girl?' Carolle said it had been a girl and she had died from what is called a 'cot death'. She said that Jean had confirmed what she felt deep inside: 'I just knew that my baby had come back to me and was growing again inside me.' She added that she had not mentioned this feeling to anyone, even her husband, for fear of being thought 'funny'. She was very worried that the tragedy of losing her first baby might happen again. Jean reassured her that her grandmother had promised everything would be fine, and she must now look forward with confidence and happiness to the 're-birth' of her intended daughter. Jean said she need not accept the offer of a test to tell the sex of the baby as she now knew the answer.

Shortly afterwards Jean came into the kitchen and asked if

I could bring some coffee into the sitting room. She said that Carolle was asking questions about babies and children passing to the spirit world and that I could help in answering some of the questions. As I came into the room I heard Carolle say to Jean, 'So you believe in reincarnation?' We said that reincarnation is a major philosophical basis for some religions and that it made sense to us. I said that in the case of Carolle's baby, for example, there had been a physical mistake or accident that had occurred in the body that her daughter's spirit had chosen. When a new healthy physical body had been conceived, the spirit of her daughter had returned to the new body to fulfil its destiny to live her life with the parents it was intended she should have. I said that I also believed that, following a full-length physical life, a spirit can return for further physical lives to gain experience and knowledge. Some people refer to this as working out one's Kharma.

Carolle said we had also answered another question she had wondered about, which is when does a spirit enter the physical body. I said that in Carolle's example her daughter's spirit entered the new foetus at conception. I stressed that this was not always the case: in a miscarriage, for example, the spirit of the baby often returns to the spirit world and begins its progression in spirit. We call this spirit a 'pure spirit', as it has not been influenced by our physical world. Jean said that our spirit friends had told us that a spirit which could not remain in an imperfect foetus might return at the next conception and live a full physical life. This was the first example of the phenomenon we had met, and we were as pleased to share the experience as Carolle was to know her daughter had returned.

The very same week another woman came to see Jean. Almost immediately Jean saw a beautiful little girl sitting next to her. She then heard two adults who said: 'Tell Pat we are taking good care of Sarah, and she is happy and well.' Jean passed on this message, adding, 'I feel your grandparents are taking care of your daughter. Your daughter and grandparents are in spirit, aren't they?' The woman said that her daughter's name was indeed Sarah and that both she and her grandparents were in spirit.

'You know your daughter is here with us now, don't you? I can see her so clearly.'

Pat said that she knew her daughter was present as she could always feel her presence, but had never seen her.

Jean then looked puzzled. 'Sarah is talking to me and says she is learning to swim, and that she is not blue any more.'

Pat broke down and began to cry. When she composed herself she explained that Sarah had passed at the age of three as the result of a hole in the heart. When Pat bathed her she would play happily for hours, splashing about. Pat said she knew Sarah would have loved to go to the swimming baths but because of her condition it would have been dangerous.

Jean then talked of how Sarah followed Pat round the garden helping her and that she was holding a huge bunch of daisies and buttercups. Pat said Sarah was always picking the daisies and buttercups from the lawn to give her. Sarah then spoke of when she would meet her mummy in the spirit world. Pat said she was upset not to be able to share the experience of Sarah growing up. Jean said Sarah had a lovely message for her: 'I will grow and progress in the spirit world, but when we meet you will be as you are now and I will be as you remember me when I passed. We will then grow together through the life we should have had in a matter of seconds.'

As Pat couldn't understand what had been said, Jean explained. 'When a baby or young child passes to the spirit world he or she continues to grow. In this life a child passes through various physical stages of growth, at the same time acquiring knowledge and maturity. In spirit this growth is purely spiritual and mental, without the physical change. As time is only relevant to the physical world, time does not exist in spirit. Although Sarah may be very wise and spiritually highly enlightened when you meet, she can show herself to you in any guise she chooses. She will appear to you exactly as you remember her now. Then in an instant you will together share all your mutual growing. When you meet in the spirit world you will have the ability to show yourself to Sarah as you are now. Your spirits will unite in harmony and love, and the experience of your child's growth will be relived together.'

Pat said what a wonderful experience to look forward to. She added how lucky Jean was to have such understanding of life in the spirit world. 'It must give you so much comfort and reassurance in your life.'

Jean said that this was one of the reasons I had written my books. 'If we can share the knowledge we have gained from our spirit friends of life in the spirit world, we hope that it may bring the comfort and strength to others that it has given us. I can help people like you in private sittings or at public demonstrations, but Bob's books will reach a far greater number of people, and give that help and comfort to a larger audience.'

Pat said that since Sarah's passing she had become involved in a children's playgroup. Although working with children who constantly reminded her of her own loss tore her apart, she felt she could give to other children the love she would have given Sarah. Jean said how very brave and unselfish Pat was, and she must now realise that Sarah was always close to her and helping her in this work. 'Sarah has just said that she knew she was going to die, and so did you.' Pat said this was absolutely true, and the short time they had together was wonderful. Pat now knew that she had so much to look forward to when she was to meet Sarah once again in spirit.

As Pat was leaving Jean said she should look at the lawn this summer. Sarah had said that there would be an extra amount of daisies and buttercups this year, which was Sarah's way of continuing to give her mummy her little bunches of flowers. I asked Pat if she would mind me using her lovely story in the book, and she said it would be nice to share it with as many people as possible and she hoped it might bring comfort to anyone experiencing the anguish of losing their young child.

But Jean's gift has not just benefited other people. It has also

helped us enormously when we have mourned the death of a
loved one.

Jean had a very special relationship with her grandmother.
When Jean was very young she joined a dance group. 'Gran'
went too, and when the group toured the country for compe-
titions Gran always went with Jean. Jean's parents were both
working full time, so she spent more time with her grandmother
than with anyone, and over the years they became very close.
Even after we got married Gran visited us every week. Although
this meant her getting several buses, we always had our visit
from Gran every Wednesday, no matter how bad the weather
was.

When we adopted the children Gran was so excited to see
her great-grandchildren each week. We all loved her dearly and
often we took her on holiday with us, which she loved. In the
summer the children would often suggest that we take Gran
for a ride in the car. One such day, as we were driving along,
I noticed a hump-backed bridge. I winked at Jean and went a
little quicker. As the car shot over the bridge I looked in the
mirror and saw Gran leave the back seat. She shot up in the air
and her false teeth flew out. I stopped the car and we were all
laughing, including Gran. I apologised but Gran said it was
marvellous and could we do it again. As she smiled and spoke
through her gummy mouth we were all in hysterics, especially
watching the children scratching about trying to find Gran's
teeth.

By this time Jean and I had begun our work for spirit,
so when we were out at lectures and services Gran always
volunteered to babysit for us. As the years passed and the
children grew older we no longer needed Gran's services as a
babysitter. By now Gran was ninety years old. We put it to her
that the children were old enough to take care of themselves
while we were out on our work for spirit, but we could sense
how upset she was thinking that she had become useless in her
old age. So we decided that we would continue to ask Gran to
babysit, knowing in fact that the roles had been reversed. When

we had an engagement for spirit, it was the children who were 'granny-sitting'. They never went to bed until we had arrived home, when Gran as usual gave us a report on the children. We could see how pleased she was to feel that she was still doing a useful and important job. You can imagine how close to our hearts we and the children held Gran. We were devastated when at the age of ninety-seven she had two severe strokes that left her unable to speak and almost completely blind. She was also nearly stone deaf.

We gave Gran healing and passed her name to all our friends who were healers. All of the churches we served put Gran's name on their absent healing list. Whenever we took a service at a church we always had to give an update on Gran's health, as so many people were genuinely concerned for this dear old lady.

One day, having seen Gran only a few days before, we walked into Jean's parents' living room, where Gran had always lived. She was seated in her own chair as usual. As we came into the room she turned and her face lit up as she spoke to Jean. Gran could see us, she had heard us come in, and she could speak. What an advertisement for 'absent healing'. We told all our friends and the churches about Gran's remarkable recovery, and everyone was as happy as we were. Gran had always been a marvellous knitter, knitting jumpers and scarves for the whole family. She began to make a hedgehog, and it was entered in a competition organised by the Shropshire old people's welfare council. The hedgehog won first prize and Gran received a diploma of merit signed by the chairman of the council. Can you imagine the joy this gave a lady of ninety-seven who some months before had suffered two massive strokes? Jean has this certificate today, and no amount of money on earth would come even near to the value we put on it.

Sadly Gran was soon to take a turn for the worse. She suffered a further series of strokes and became very ill indeed. She lost all her speech again and was virtually blind. But just before they took Gran into hospital for the last time I was privileged to share an extraordinary event that occurred between her and Jean.

By now everyone knew that Gran was dying, even Gran herself. She kept asking Jean: 'Why won't they let me go?' Jean more than anyone was suffering every moment that her grandmother was in pain. It was at this time that publication of my first book was due. We were attending meetings in London regularly, but Jean had made it clear that no matter how important a meeting might be or where we might be if we received an urgent telephone call from Jean's parents, we would drop everything without question and return home immediately.

We went to see Gran the day before she was to be taken into hospital. She was lying in bed, and Jean and I were very upset as we looked down on our dearest friend in such a pitiful state. Jean knelt down and held Gran's hand, then she put her mouth next to Gran's ear and whispered something. Jean sat back and waited. Suddenly a remarkable change took place in Gran's whole personality. I can only describe it by saying that it was as if Gran was 'shining': her eyes began to sparkle and she began to smile.

Jean started to talk to Gran about the times they had spent together when Jean was very young. Gran talked quite easily and referred to names and places that held special memories for them both. There was laughter and joy as the two relived their private and treasured memories. Gran was lucid and responsive to the conversation. I couldn't believe what was happening until the truth suddenly dawned on me. Jean had in some way reached 'the spirit of Grandma': her spirit had projected itself through the tired and physically inhibiting body. I was witnessing a purely spiritual conversation. This lasted for about twenty minutes until I sensed the 'glow' around Gran beginning to fade. Slowly she returned to the sad, deaf, blind and very old-looking lady we had seen on entering the room. As the last embers of spiritual light faded Jean whispered 'Goodbye, Gran,' and we left the room.

Three days later Gran passed to the spirit world. The funeral was on a Monday, the day Jean normally does private sittings. Jean phoned her sitters to ask if they could come on another day. Some of them were very put out, even when Jean explained the circumstances, so she said that she would see the sitters on Monday night.

The funeral was a very moving experience and Jean was as emotional as anyone. You might think that because of her work as a medium and the thousands of messages she has given from loved ones in spirit Jean would not react as a 'normal' person in these circumstances. The loss of a loved one such as Gran, however, affects a medium in exactly the same way as it does anyone else. Jean was shattered by the loss of physical contact with her Gran, and by the fact that she could no longer hold her and kiss her. After the funeral Jean had to get her thoughts together in order to give four private sittings, within hours of paying her last respects to one of the people she loved most dearly. I doubt whether the sitters that night understood the pressure she was under, although with extra help from her spirit friends she honoured her commitments.

Jean sent out many thoughts to Gran and her spirit friends for confirmation that her grandmother had arrived safely in the spirit world. She received no response from either source for some days. We were driving to take a meeting in Birmingham, both deep in private thoughts preparing for the evening meeting. Suddenly I heard Jean give a very loud gasp and saw her thrown heavily back into her seat. She said loudly, 'Oh my God,' and instantly broke down and cried uncontrollably. I stopped the car and put my arms round her, wondering what on earth had happened. When she calmed down she explained what had happened.

'I was talking to Henry and Lucy, asking for help in the meeting tonight. Suddenly another voice came through loud and clear. *It was Gran's voice.* She repeated the words I had whispered to her the last time I saw her before she died, "I love you", then her spirit passed through me. We became one spirit. Now I know that Gran will be with me for ever.' Now it was my turn to shed tears as I thanked Gran for showing us she was safe and well. I know that Gran is part of Jean and always will be.

You may have noticed that this book is dedicated to a single person. I feel that no further explanation is necessary.

Chapter Six

Just a Job

Jean and I have never been reluctant to tell anyone of our involvement with spirit if we are asked. This has led to some varied responses, however. We had been shopping in Shrewsbury one day and as we were leaving the shop a woman stopped us and asked if we could spare her a few minutes. She explained that she was conducting a survey of people's shopping habits, and began by asking us the sort of items we had purchased and why we had chosen particular brands. She then asked if we would object to answering questions about the sort of work we did. I said that I was a tool-maker in a local engineering factory and that I had been doing this type of work all my life. The researcher then asked Jean if she worked and Jean replied very casually that she was a medium. The woman wrote it down and then looked up in amazement. 'You did say a *medium*, you work as a medium?' Jean said that was correct and gave a brief description of the sort of demonstrations she gives. The woman became very excited. 'That's incredible. In all the time I've been doing this job you are the first medium I've ever met. It can get very boring as most people have ordinary sorts of jobs, but to meet a medium – it's great. Thank you for stopping. You have really made my day. Just wait till my friends hear about this; they will be dead jealous of me. Do you give private sittings as well?' Jean handed her one of her cards and she went off very excited. She later came to see Jean with two friends.

As Jean explained to the market researcher, mediumship is now her job. In any job, as we all know, we meet different people, some of whom we like and others we do not. Jean is no exception. She is meeting new people all the time in sittings and at public demonstrations. She has to put personal feelings towards people she may not like to the back of her mind, for these feelings must not be allowed to affect her work for spirit. At times this can be a very difficult exercise. Jean also constantly changes the presentation of her mediumship to suit the different people seeking her services. Despite this she has never changed her natural personality, no matter whom she may be addressing or from what background the person comes. Her motto is simple: take me as I am or not at all.

Initially, Jean only did demonstrations in spiritualist churches but after a few years we felt we wanted to reach a wider audience. Once again our spirit friends were aware of our thoughts and soon responded to our wishes.

We had finished a service one day at the Morris Hall in Shrewsbury. As we sat drinking our coffee two young girls came up to us and asked if we ever spoke and demonstrated anywhere other than in spiritualist churches. We said that we had been considering for some time how we could share our knowledge and experiences outside the confines of churches. The girls said they had invited Clifford (who was the president of Shrewsbury church) to talk to their group on mediumship and spiritualism, but he could not come on the night they had mentioned and suggested they ask us instead. The girls said they were members of the 'Eighteen Plus' group at Dawley, and the group met one night each week at the Elephant and Castle public house. We said we would be delighted to talk to them and looked forward to discussing the subject with young people. That was the opening we had been looking for, and it was the beginning of many years' speaking to many different organisations not associated with the spiritualist religion.

We love talking to younger people especially, for they are never afraid to express their scepticism openly. Most groups of young people hold their meetings in public houses. The two most popular groups to invite us to their meetings were the Eighteen Plus and the Young Farmers, both of which met in their local pubs. You may feel that Jean and I might have been reluctant to talk on spiritual matters in the atmosphere of a public house, but the venues had one important advantage for us. We were taking the subject of our talks and demonstrations to the young people's home territory. They felt safe there, and were more relaxed and comfortable, which had the effect of producing very lively and enthusiastic meetings. We feel that if we had invited the young groups to the churches, it would have created an inhibiting atmosphere.

The normal time these young people's meetings close is around nine-thirty, which allows the members time to have a drink before the pubs close. (Beer is strictly forbidden during the meetings.) Once I have addressed the group and Jean has given a short demonstration, we leave the rest of the meeting open for questions and answers. Every single time the meeting has continued until well past closing time, without the members asking to leave for a drink. On many occasions it has been Jean and I who have asked if they would excuse us as it was getting late. There is immense interest shown by young people in the subject and their questions are always direct and probing. They do not suffer fools lightly and they demand sensible answers, and we love this as it keeps us on our toes and instils an attitude of common sense and serious investigation. We recommend all mediums working on public platforms to follow our example and take the subject and themselves out from the churches to the young enquiring minds. Obviously we also enjoy speaking and demonstrating in churches and spiritualist groups, but there the challenge is not as acute, for you are addressing people who in the majority have accepted the philosophy and principles of mediumship and spiritualism.

There has only been one occasion when, at a Young Farmers meeting, a young man made his scepticism openly visible to all present. During my talk I could see him giggling and sighing and generally disturbing his friends sitting close to him. When Jean stood up to begin her talk and demonstration, Henry, Jean's spirit friend, directed her straight to this young man. I smiled to myself, knowing from experience that this was exactly how Henry operates. Jean spoke to him. 'To begin my demonstration of what Bob has been talking about I would like to come to the young man who obviously finds our presence here amusing and boring.' This was followed by a spontaneous round of applause from the rest of the members. The young man sat with a very embarrassed smile on his face while Jean continued. 'Your father is talking to me. He passed with a heart attack and his passing came as a great shock to all the family. He says he is not pleased with the progress you are making with your studies. He tells me you have had to sit your exams for the second time.' There was a positive response from his friends who were nodding their heads towards Jean, and the young man's face had changed from the cynical smile to one of amazement. 'Who's Derek?' Jean asked. The young man answered in a very humble voice that Derek was his name. 'Your father asked me to tell Derek he is not very proud of your behaviour. He says you would do well to follow his example. He was a very polite and kind person; I get the feeling that he was a true gentleman. Your father is asking me to ask you to take care of your mother, as she has been ill and needs your attention. He says he has your dog with him and they are happy together. Your dog was a lovely red setter; I can see him quite clearly.' The change in the young man's attitude was remarkable. I began to feel sorry for him, as it was obvious Jean had touched a very sore point with his dog. When Jean moved on to give someone else a message, we noticed the young man make a quiet and unobtrusive exit. When Jean finished her demonstration and we moved on to the questions and answers, Jean asked if one of Derek's friends would go and see that he was all right. The friend soon returned and said that Derek was drowning his embarrassment with the other sorts of spirit at the bar downstairs. We spoke to Derek afterwards and he apologised for his behaviour. He said the accuracy of Jean's message for him was incredible, and it had shaken him to the core. About two years later we were invited back to this particular group to repeat our talk and demonstration; Derek was again present but on this occasion his behaviour was impeccable.

Some of the organisations we have spoken to include the Inner Wheel, Rotary clubs, professional and business ladies' clubs, Tangent clubs, youth clubs and housewives' groups. One day I received a phone call from the secretary of a ladies' luncheon club. She said they had speakers at their monthly luncheons and asked if we would be interested in joining them for lunch followed by a talk and demonstration. She gave me the date and the venue of their meeting. Her voice gave me the impression of distinct affluence, and this was confirmed when she mentioned the venue – an inn noted for its high standards and prices. When I told Jean where we were going for lunch she said, 'Blimey, I'll have to wear my best clothes and brush up my table manners!'

On the day of our luncheon engagement we arrived at the inn and were shown into the lounge, where we were introduced to the secretary. We were asked what we would like to drink, and I asked for a white wine while Jean said she would have her favourite, Britvic orange mixed with lemonade. The secretary looked surprised and said Jean must have something stronger. Jean said she didn't like spirits – quickly adding it was only the sort that came out of bottles that she didn't like.

The secretary said she wanted to introduce us to some of the other members before we sat down for lunch. The first person we were introduced to was the local lady Mayoress, who was wearing her chain of office. After some polite conversation we were introduced to other members who seemed to be trying to give a self-important image. Eventually we were escorted to the 'top' table and seated next to the lady Mayoress and the officials of the club. Jean was next to me.

The first course was soup. Jean hates any sort of soup, and declined the offer. When we are working for spirit we never feel at all hungry before we start. The nerves and the preparation are so intense that it completely ruins the appetite. We had often been in a similar situation at a luncheon club or evening meeting when the group would eat first and then we would talk and demonstrate afterwards, and we have missed some great meals because of this. But we always feel ravenous after we have worked, which I think is due to the amount of nervous energy we burn off during the demonstration. I could not count the times we have refused some super food, only to stop off at the nearest chippie on our way home from a meeting and sat thoroughly enjoying fish and chips in the car dressed in our best clothes. Jean has often smiled and said, 'I wonder what the people I have just demonstrated to would say if they could see us now.'

When the main course was served it was glorious – roast beef and Yorkshire pudding with all the trimmings. I knew this was Jean's favourite but she could only eat a very small portion for the sake of politeness. After the dessert, coffee and chocolates were served, then brandy and other sweeties.

During lunch Jean had whispered to me how uncomfortable she was in the present company. It was not that she felt inferior in any way, but that the whole atmosphere was false. I said I felt exactly the same, and it had been confirmed during the meal. All the ladies on our table went to great lengths to tell the others where they had spent their summer holidays in the most exotic places, how they had had their houses modernised, how they could not get used to the new car, and how 'tiresome' it was holding dinner parties for their husbands' influential guests. Jean and I both sensed that the main object of their meetings was simply to try to outdo or impress their fellow-members.

One lady in particular had been demonstrating this attitude more strongly than the others. During lunch she asked me whereabouts in Telford we lived. I said we lived on Woodside. 'I've heard of Woodside, but surely that's a council estate, isn't it?' I said yes, that was correct, and that we lived in a council house. After nearly choking on her croûtons, she treated us as if we had brought the plague with us. She said that she did not know how anyone could live in such a place, and she always felt relieved when she passed through Telford to have come out safely. I explained that not everyone has freedom of choice as to where to live. I said that most of our closest friends lived in council houses in Telford and that they were the kindest and most considerate people you could wish to meet. I added that we had raised our two children in Telford and they were now adults and we felt we had achieved a great deal in the town.

I noticed that Jean had overheard the conversation and had that look of anger on her face. I knew that she was about to erupt so I defused the situation by asking who had been invited recently to their lunches. Fortunately it was soon time for our talk. I deliberately used a topic which I expressed very strongly, namely the lack of spiritual thoughts and actions and the obsessive preoccupation with material gain in the world today. Jean gave a very short demonstration and we then made excuses to leave as quickly as possible. The secretary said we would receive our fee from the treasurer and took us to the very lady who had been so offensive at lunch. I turned round and walked away. I could not bring myself to speak to her and be made to feel that I was going cap in hand for our fee. Jean said she would meet me outside, so I said goodbye and it was a lovely feeling to breathe the fresh air and be away from the atmosphere we had endured.

As we set off for home I asked Jean if anything had been said. She smiled and said that when the treasurer had asked her what our fee was, Jean had doubled our normal charge. She said she knew it was wrong but she couldn't help it when she realised who the treasurer was. She said she hoped Henry and Lucy would understand and forgive her. I said that knowing Lucy she would be having a good laugh and probably saying it serves them right. We had a pub lunch later on the strength of our 'extra' fee.

A few weeks later we were invited to the Welshpool ladies' group for a similar meeting. The comparison between the two restored our faith in ladies' groups. When we arrived at the venue, the Church House in Welshpool, we were given a very warm welcome by the secretary, who said how much they were looking forward to the evening. They had arranged for the local newspaper to come along and take pictures, and a report of the evening would appear in the paper. She explained that all the members had got together and prepared a buffet supper, and asked whether we would prefer to eat before or after our talk and demonstration. The whole atmosphere was one of consideration towards us, and was very friendly and harmonious.

We were then introduced to the vicar's wife. The Church House belonged to the Church of England, and knowing how the orthodox church felt towards spiritualism I had wondered what sort of reception we might receive. I asked if the vicar would be attending our meeting and his wife said that he had felt it would be inappropriate on account of his belief. She said that tonight was the night the church bell-ringers normally held their bell-ringing practice, but her husband had cancelled the practice as it might disturb our meeting. I asked if she would thank the vicar for his kind thought and say how sorry we were not to have the opportunity of meeting him. I said I knew we would have had a very interesting discussion comparing our individual beliefs and religions.

In any form of communication with spirit, one only receives according to what one is prepared to give. The Welshpool meeting was a resounding success, and Jean's demonstration was brilliant. The members had put a lot of effort into making us feel welcome and by doing so had made spirit feel welcome also. Spirit in return gave of their best and many members received wonderful communication. It proved to us once again how sensitive spirit are to atmosphere. At the previous ladies' club we had found it very difficult to work because of the members' self-absorbed, arrogant attitude. Spirit had also re-acted to this atmosphere and it was difficult for them to get close to Jean.

Jean has sitters who come from all walks of life: some are business people and some are obviously very well off. Without exception everyone has commented on the warm, friendly atmosphere they feel in our home. Jean has never felt that the position a person holds or his background or wealth was important; it is the person himself who is important, not his status. Jean has now accepted totally that people come to see *her*, to share her remarkable gift. They respect her for her work, and where or how we live is of no importance to them. Her initial self-consciousness about living on a council estate was soon removed by the obvious joy she could see her gift bringing to people from all sections of the community.

One man in particular who came for a sitting gave me quite a shock in this respect. As I spoke to him in the kitchen before taking him to see Jean, he said he hoped his car would not cause an obstruction: he had parked it outside our garage but it was sticking out into the road. I was curious to know how any car could stick out into the road from the space in front of the garage, so when he went into the sitting room I went up to the garage and carefully opened the door. I was greeted by the sight of a new Rolls-Royce Silver Cloud parked outside. It was obvious that the planners had not allowed for such a car to be parked outside our council house.

Another businessman came to see Jean with his friend, Bill, who had come along to keep him company. Bill had openly expressed his scepticism to me in the kitchen while his friend was having his sitting. When Bill went in for his sitting I wondered how Jean would get on. I should not have worried: Bill came out with red eyes. His father had come through and given him excellent evidence. He explained that he had been considering expanding his engineering company but professional advisers had urged against it. Bill was wondering if Jean would pick up this situation and was interested in how she might advise him. Bill's father had spoken through Jean about this expansion and told Bill that he had hesitated for far too long. He should go immediately to the bank and begin the business of securing a loan and get on with plans for the expansion. Bill explained that this would mean taking out a second mortgage on his house and having a massive overdraft at the bank, but he said he was so impressed with his sitting and the evidence that his father had given – his father had been a brilliant businessman and any advice he offered Bill was confident would be sound – that he would begin the process of negotiating the loans straight away.

When Bill and his friend left, Jean repeated what she has said to me many times: 'Oh God, I hope it works out right. I know spirit has never let me down but it's such a responsibility passing on spirit's advice. It could change a person's whole way of life for better or worse. I'm still here in the physical body should spirit's advice not work out. It's me they will come back to.' This is one reason I am glad that I am not gifted with the ability to see or hear spirit. When I speak in public or private on the mechanics and philosophy of mediumship and spiritualism, people have the option to say either 'That's true and makes sense' or 'What a load of rubbish'. I do not have the responsibility that Jean holds on her shoulders when offering personal advice to people from spirit.

Jean has said that if ever she passed on advice from spirit that resulted in anyone being harmed or hurt, she would close the door once again to spirit and *never* reopen it. In all the time she has been working as a medium, this fear has never materialised. Jean has given her spirit friends this ultimatum and we know that they have respected her wishes. She still has this feeling of responsibility, however, and we believe this is good, for some mediums adopt the attitude: 'Well, it was spirit that said that, not me. Don't blame me, blame spirit.' Jean is responsible for *all* that takes place, even though she is only the channel for spirit.

Bill has been back to see Jean on several occasions since his first sitting and received further advice from his father. A fitting finale to this episode was when Bill came to see Jean to ask if she could give him a new name for the company, as it had become very successful following his father's advice. The name Jean received from spirit was 'Phoenix'. Bill laughed out loud, saying that was typical of his father: he had been cremated, 'and he obviously knew of my scepticism when I first came to see you. He has really "risen from the ashes" to help and advise me.' The name may be common in business circles, but only Bill and we know how significant his company name really is.

Jean and I are often asked to use our gifts when we least expect it. We were having lunch at our local pub when the owner came over to talk to us. She said that her sister was in terrible pain as the result of a slipped disc: she was unable to help in the pub because of the pain and for the past weeks had been confined to a chair. The owner had read that I was a healer and asked if she could make an appointment for her sister to see me. I said there was no need to make an appointment as I could give her sister healing after we had finished our meal.

We were taken through the bar and upstairs to the private living quarters. We knew the woman well as she had served us many times during our regular meals in the lounge. She was seated in the chair and it was obvious that she was in very severe pain. I explained as always that I could not promise to heal her but that I would try. I asked if she had ever had healing before, and she replied that she hadn't. I said that I would simply place my hands on the area where the pain was and that she should try to relax and think of something pleasant.

After the healing was finished I told the woman not to expect any miracles; it was usual that relief from pain and discomfort was gradual but I felt that we had been successful. She said that she had experienced a very strange feeling during the

73

healing, as if there was an electric fire near her back and a lovely warm sensation in the area of my hands.

The next week when we went again for lunch I was surprised to see her serving behind the bar. She put her thumb up to me as we sat down. She came across to the table and said that she had never slept so well as she did the night following the healing, and the very next day she had been able to walk about and the pain had almost gone. Within a couple of days she was back in the lounge working as normal. She asked me how much she owed me for the healing. I explained that I have never charged a penny for healing and never will. The joy of seeing her back at work was reward enough.

One day Jean was rushed into hospital following a very serious attack of angina. She spent two days in the intensive care unit while various tests were carried out. When the doctors were sure that it was not a heart attack she was moved into an ordinary ward. One of the sisters came to talk to Jean about the profession she had read on her form. She asked if it was true that she was a medium. Jean talked for some time, explaining her gifts and the type of work she did for spirit. The news spread very quickly and Jean told me when I visited her that she had spent most of the day talking to the nurses and doctors and giving short sittings to some of them. She said it was amazing how interested the staff were about mediumship, and added jokingly that she would be glad to get home for a rest.

Jean always has her hair done at Michael's hairdressing shop in Okengates. On many occasions the whole shop has come to a standstill, with customers and staff crowded round Jean asking her questions and booking appointments for private sittings.

But of all the thousands of people we have met as the result of Jean's mediumship no one made such an impression on me as a man named Frank.

When I arranged the appointment the man said he would be

arriving with two friends who would also like to have sittings with Jean. From the conversation I had no indication of what to expect when the three of them arrived. I answered the door on the evening of the appointment to find a lady and gentleman accompanied by another gentleman in a wheelchair. They asked if the wheelchair would be a nuisance and I said not at all. Frank, the man in the wheelchair, had elected to see Jean first. His friends wheeled him into the sitting room and then returned for coffee in the kitchen. When his sitting was over Jean wheeled Frank into the kitchen, then his two friends went in together for their sitting.

I moved one of the chairs so that Frank could draw up to the kitchen table. For me to describe him as being severely disabled would be an understatement; it was obvious that he was suffering from acute cerebral palsy. Out of habit I asked if he would like tea or coffee and then realised that it would be very difficult for him to hold the cup steady. He must have sensed my embarrassment but said he would love a cup of tea, and asked if I would excuse him if he used a straw to drink it with. I said not at all and we sat down at the table. I asked if he had enjoyed his sitting. Frank said that it had been wonderful, and how marvellous it must be for Jean to have been born with her gifts.

Nervously I asked about his condition. He told me not to feel embarrassed as he had had a lifetime's experience of talking about it. He explained that he had grown up with his disability and was now hardened to the cruel and snide remarks that were made about him, especially by children. He now ignored such comments, feeling more sorry for those making them than for himself. I asked if he had any hobbies or interests, and he replied that he wished he had the time for such things. I was curious as to how he passed his time, being so severely disabled. He said that for some years he had worked at a factory but a few years ago he had opened a centre for severely disabled people, training them to use light engineering machinery such as presses, and had obtained some contracts to supply parts to various companies. This helped to finance the venture and so enable more disabled people to receive help.

Frank explained that the object of his scheme was twofold. He felt it was important to give severely disabled people such as himself a feeling of achievement by doing something worth while and contributing to the community in some way. He felt it gave them more confidence in themselves, and encouraged them to take on more challenges should the opportunity arise. Frank said he was also busy visiting factories in the area, speaking to managers and trying to educate them into accepting disabled persons into their companies, explaining the many jobs disabled people were capable of doing. He said that together with local councillors he had approached central government officials and they were now monitoring similar schemes nationwide. He felt very proud that he had personally found full-time employment for a number of severely disabled people in various jobs.

I was fascinated listening to this man and became aware of a feeling of great humility in his presence. I was in the company of a man so disabled he could not even hold a cup of tea, yet he was so busy helping other people in the same predicament that he had no time for hobbies or feeling sorry for himself. I could have understood if he had felt bitter or resentful at the blow life had dealt him, but instead he was using his own disability to bring hope and inspiration to those in similar circumstances.

I asked Frank what had led him to make an appointment to see Jean. He said that from a very early age he had been aware of the spirituality within us and that he had always known that deep inside himself there was a healthy, lively spirit. He had received tremendous help and support from spirit in the past, and when friends had mentioned Jean to him he felt he should come and meet her. He said he knew that one day his spirit would be released from the disability of his human body and would then have the total freedom of the spirit world. I told him how impressed I was that, far from allowing his disability to inhibit what he did, he was leading an active life that a fully able-bodied person would find fulfilling.

The short time I was privileged to be in Frank's company made such an impact on me that I shall never forget it. I felt that he was an example to us all. Often we tend to feel sorry for ourselves when faced with difficulties, and some of us become bitter and angry if we feel life has been unkind to us. I hope that if ever I find myself feeling that way I can remember Frank, for I know his example will give me the inspiration and courage to face whatever life should hold in store. I wish him every success in his endeavours and I know that spirit will be supporting and helping a very brave man.

Chapter Seven

Misconceptions

As with any other job, Jean would be the first to admit that as a medium she can make mistakes. If the communication is not as clear as she would like, it is possible that she may interpret what she thinks she has heard incorrectly. But when Jean is certain that the message she receives from spirit is correct, and she has followed a process of rechecking with spirit, she will not change the message even though the recipient may argue strongly that it is wrong. Jean's favourite comment in this situation is: 'Well, love, I *know* I'm right. I can't change what spirit has given me because you feel that you can't accept it. Promise me that when I am proved right you will contact me and I will accept your apology.' This is always said with good humour and usually accepted in the same manner.

Janet had been working in the offices at the same company as I. She had spoken to me many times about Jean's gift as a medium, saying how interesting she found the subject. After many questions she asked me if I would arrange a private sitting for her with Jean. I did this, after explaining to Janet that I never discuss with Jean beforehand anything I might know about a person who has made an appointment. When Janet arrived for her sitting the only thing Jean knew about her was that she worked at the same company as myself. This has been the situation on many occasions when a work colleague or an acquaintance of mine has booked a sitting with Jean. I always send a little prayer to spirit asking that Jean may receive good evidence, so that when I meet my colleagues after their sitting they are satisfied that all went well. This has always proved the case, until Janet came to see me in the stores the day after her sitting with Jean.

She asked me if she could have a private word about her sitting with Jean, and I could see that she looked very concerned about something. She asked me if Jean ever made mistakes with the messages she gives. I said that at public demonstrations I had seen Jean give messages to people who accepted all that she had said. Jean would, however, mention to me that she was not happy with the communication and had the feeling something was not quite right about it. After the meeting a different person would come to Jean privately and say, 'I'm sorry, Jean, but I *knew* that was *my* father (or mother or whoever had been communicating), and everything he (or she) said was right. I felt too embarrassed to put my hand up and question who you were talking to.' Jean always thanks the person for confirming her niggling doubt, adding that although she had spoken to someone else, as long as the person whom she should have been speaking to knew the message was for them, then their friend or relative in spirit would also know, and would be happy. I said that at a private sitting this could obviously never happen, as there is only a one-to-one relationship. Then the practice of 'body-snatching' – the term we use to describe people who try to grab messages that are for someone else – is impossible. (It is interesting to note that a good medium can normally sense the presence of 'body snatchers' by the way they respond. They usually agree with everything the medium says, and give no sign of questioning. The word 'no' is never part of their vocabulary.)

Janet said that she was very pleased with the evidence Jean had given from her father. She had no doubt at all that her father was communicating through Jean, for Jean had mentioned names and personal details that only she herself and her father could possibly have known. What was worrying her was part of the message that referred to her moving house. Her father had told Jean that Janet would soon be moving to the south. Janet had questioned Jean about this, saying that they had only recently bought their house and were very happy where they were. She and her husband had good jobs and the children were settled in school. Janet had told Jean that there was no way they would be moving south: they had no family or connections in the south, so Jean must have got it wrong.

After what Janet told me I could only agree with how she felt, and strange as it might seem to me, knowing Jean's record of reliability, I said that I would check with Jean and tell Janet the next day. When I asked Jean about Janet's concern she said that she had simply passed on what Janet's father had said. Jean would not change her message, but told me to tell Janet that spirit would not have told her about the move if it wasn't right. I passed on Jean's comments, adding that it would be best for Janet to forget about the move, and if it happened – so be it.

Some weeks later Janet came to see me in the stores. She was very upset and began to explain what had happened. She had heard that week that her husband had been given notice of his intended redundancy. The company for whom he worked, however, had said that they could make an exception in his case and arrange a transfer to their parent company in the south of England. Janet had previously mentioned Jean's message to her husband but he had been very sceptical about the whole subject. Following this development he had now asked Janet to get Jean once again to confirm that it was right for them to accept this move. Jean said she was sorry about the circumstances that had caused her message from Janet's father to be proved correct, but that they should accept the offer. We have since heard from Janet that she and the family have settled in Bristol, where things are looking good for them. She thanked Jean for sticking to her guns over the message to move, saying that when the announcement of her husband's redundancy was made, the shock was softened by the knowledge that her father had advised them to accept the move.

Jean was halfway through another private sitting when she suddenly turned to the woman and asked if she was worried about a friend in hospital. The woman replied that her brother had been taken into hospital for surgery but was recovering and was expected home very soon. Jean asked the woman if she would telephone the hospital the moment she got home. When the woman asked why, Jean simply replied: 'I feel it is important that you should.'

The following day Jean received a telephone call from the woman saying that she had arrived home to learn that the family and the hospital had been trying to find her. She had felt reluctant to tell anyone that she had made an appointment with Jean, so they hadn't known where to contact her. At the exact time Jean had passed on her feelings about telephoning the hospital, the brother had unexpectedly died.

Jean has been asked many times if she is ever told or has ever predicted the death of someone. She always answers that she feels this would not be allowed, and in twenty years of working as a medium this particular occasion is as close as she has come to doing so. In this case it was not a prediction, for she simply received from spirit a sense of importance surrounding the telephone call to the hospital at precisely the time the man had passed. Why she should have received such a feeling at that exact moment is open to speculation.

Mrs Godstone had been seeing Jean for many years as a regular sitter. She and her husband lived in a mobile home and were finding life very hard. They came to see Jean not for evidence of life after death, but to ask advice from spirit as to what they might do to help improve their standard of living. Mrs Godstone's father had been a regular communicator at previous sittings, and on this occasion she was advised that the family should move to another area. Jean said she felt that they should head for Southampton.

The family packed all their belongings into the lorry and towing their mobile home set off for Southampton. Some time later Mrs Godstone wrote to Jean, saying that things were not much better and maybe Jean had got the message wrong? Jean said she would use her tarot cards to see what feelings she got. (She occasionally uses the cards as a method of psychic divination, but only if it is impossible for the sitter to get to her, and if the problem is purely materialistic.)

Jean wrote back to Mrs Godstone saying that the tarot had only confirmed that they should remain where they were and under no account return to the Midlands. Jean added that she felt that if they moved north of Oxford something disastrous would happen. We heard much later that this advice was unheeded and as the family passed through Oxford on the journey back to Telford the engine of the lorry blew up. After a very costly repair they turned round and headed back to Southampton. There was a happy ending, however, for the family were offered a council house and Mrs Godstone's husband eventually found a steady job.

People have some strange ideas about what a medium actually does. I was still working at the factory when I was confronted by a colleague who thought mediums and spiritualists got up to some very weird practices. I had been working as a tool store-keeper for some years. My duties were to supply and record tools that were issued to the shop-floor personnel. One man who worked as a turner was a regular visitor to the stores. He knew of my involvement with spirit but his ideas of what took place, and where he got them from, are still a puzzle to me. I suppose I was guilty of not educating him to the reality of the situation, for the simple reason that at the time I felt it would have been a wasted exercise.

Whenever John came to the stores for his tools he would stand for long periods looking past me at the counter. On one occasion he had a very worried look on his face, and I asked him why he looked so concerned. 'Do you know that you are

When Jean helps the 'lost souls' who wander in the darker planes of the spirit world her work can be both frightening and dangerous.

Jean is obsessed with the Tudors and our house has become a museum to Henry VIII and his six wives. She has often communicated with Anne Boleyn.

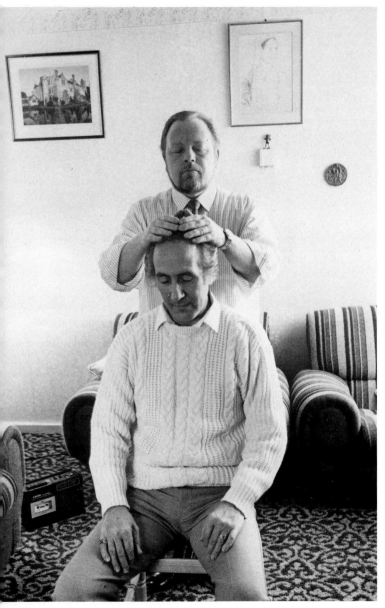

My healing powers have brought relief to many sick people.

Jean is booked up months in advance with sittings and demonstrations.

In spite of her incredible gifts, Jean still likes to think of herself as a down-to-earth housewife and mother. Here she is with our son, Andrew.

...an's powers don't yet stretch to controlling the weather . . .

...ave met an extraordinary range of people through Jean's psychic work, but ...one has impressed me more than Frank, a disabled gentleman, whose ...rage is an inspiration to us all.

Jean always had a very special relationship with her grandmother, and they still remain extremely close, even though her grandmother has passed to spirit.

henever a funeral passes by, I always remark that the funeral director's job
o put them away and Jean's job is to bring them back.

A message from the Other World reunited me with the brother I never knew I had. After a fifty-year separation, Ray and I finally met each other as a result of the publication of More To Life Than This.

in very grave danger? There are little spirits sitting on the shelves watching you.' Like a fool I turned to look into the stores while John, still very serious, continued. 'They are waiting to take control. Very soon they will overpower you.' I assumed that I was having my leg pulled, so replied that I was well aware of their presence and in fact used them to help me in my work. If someone asked for an item from the far end of the stores, all I had to do was to point my finger to the shelf and one of the 'little spirits' would rush away and fetch it for me. I soon realised, however, that John was not pulling my leg but was deadly serious. He said he was reluctant to come to the stores for he could always see these little faces looking at him. Silently I thought to myself, 'And some people say spiritualists and mediums are strange people.'

I think you will appreciate why I felt it would have been a fruitless exercise to try to explain logically how spirit really manifest themselves to a medium. Still in a calm and serious manner, John went on to explain that he knew of a house where a medium held regular seances. He said he had stood outside while the seance was taking place, and had noticed that the house was surrounded with a blue mist. Out of this blue mist he had seen the spirits gliding down and entering the house through the roof. I mentioned that we too held a development group in our house every week, and that I thought it would be a good thing if I asked the council to come and check our roof tiles: if all of our friends from the spirit world enter our house through the roof, they must be causing a lot of damage to the tiles.

I used to thank John for his concern over my welfare when he spoke of the danger I was in, but I believe he was genuinely worried for me. His remarks and obvious misguided belief about the practices of mediums are not so very startling or ridiculous compared with other theories we have been accused of indulging in. You would be amazed at what some people think mediums get up to: holding group meetings in the nude (an interesting thought, but as yet Jean and I have not been invited to hold a demonstration in a nudist camp), conducting sacrificial rites during our services, working in hand with the devil.

When Jean began her development as a medium we were recommended to make a point of seeing as many mediums working as possible. Our adviser Graham thought it important for us to see all standards of mediumship being demonstrated in public, so that Jean could learn to assess the good from the bad. 'How can you learn from the best if you haven't seen the worst?' was Graham's comment. During this period we learnt a great deal about what is genuine and what is pure theatre, and we always pass on this advice to our own groups.

We got to know one medium very well, for the simple reason that we never missed a 'performance' whenever she was booked at our local church. We now feel that it was wrong and probably she would not be asked to take services today, but at that time it seemed that she was asked purely for the entertainment value of her demonstration. I cannot mention her name as I would not wish to embarrass her: she was a dear old lady and may still be alive today. She must have been in her sixties at the time; she was very frail and had a distinctive stoop. When we reached the point in the service where she was about to address the congregation, she would sit down halfway through the hymn preceding the address to begin her preparation. When the hymn finished and the congregation sat down, the chairman would invite the medium (let's call her Mary) to give the address.

As Mary sat with her eyes closed she knew she had the undivided attention of the whole congregation. She would then begin to breathe very heavily, accompanied by groans and shaking all over. To the uninitiated it might have appeared that Mary was either in a trance or had been taken ill. Eventually she would stand up very slowly and take a few steps towards the front of the platform. If you watched closely you might see one eye pop open for a second to make sure she was standing in the right place. Suddenly would come this very deep rough voice, as if trying to impersonate a Red Indian chief in a typical John Wayne Western. On one occasion Mary got really carried away and began to turn round as 'her guide' was speaking, and she finished up talking to the wall behind her with her back to the congregation. If she happened to be facing the congregation when she finished giving her address, you would see one eye open again for a second as she slowly stepped back to sit down.

In a spiritualist service a hymn is always sung between the address and the demonstration of clairvoyance. During the hymn one's attention was drawn to Mary as she went through a reverse procedure for 'coming out of trance'. She would then be invited to give her demonstration of clairvoyance. This was always preceded by an explanation of her behaviour before, during and after the address.

'I hope you weren't worried for me during the address. I was not in any danger. My guide is a very big Red Indian chief, and as I'm only a little lady he finds it very difficult to get inside me to give his addresses.' This was always said with such sincerity that we never felt annoyed by the obvious rubbish she was talking. One evening during her demonstration of clairvoyance she came to Jean with a message. It was the only time she ever spoke to Jean, and Jean has often said since, 'Thank God it was the *only* time.' This night her message to Jean was even more entertaining than the address.

Mary said she wanted to speak to Jean as she had someone in spirit who wished to communicate with her. Whenever Mary gave a demonstration of clairvoyance it was nearly always from someone who was impossible to recognise, never a relative or a friend. Jean's message was no exception. 'There is a gentleman standing in front of you whom you should recognise. He was an old woodcutter. Does this mean anything to you?' Trying to be as co-operative as possible, Jean replied that her maiden name had been 'Wood', and maybe that might be significant. Mary's face lit up and she said, 'That's it. I knew

I was right.' Jean and I smiled to each other. Mary then delivered the following gem of a message which we have never forgotten.

'Well, my dear, he certainly gives me the impression he knows you very well, and you should recognise him because he is flashing his chopper at you. I can see the sunlight on his chopper as he waves it at you.' Well, you can imagine the reaction around the church. Most people managed to stifle their amusement but some burst out laughing loudly. Jean turned bright red with embarrassment and I had to bow my head to hide my laughter. Poor Jean didn't know where to put herself, but Mary hadn't finished yet. 'I feel he is one of your guides. He is a very strong man and will give you great power in your work. He says you will always know when he is close, for he will show you his chopper to prove it.' Well, that was the last straw and the whole congregation erupted with laughter. I have never laughed so much in my life. What made it even more amusing was that Mary just stood smiling at the congregation's reaction, obviously totally unaware of the alternative interpretation everyone had read into the message. Jean has of course never been aware of her 'woodcutter' friend and, as she has said many times since, it would have been a very unusual way for someone to identify his presence. I can't believe anyone ever took Mary's demonstrations seriously, but no one tried to persuade her to give up, for we all enjoyed her performance and she never did any harm.

When we were told that a 'psychic artist' had been booked at the church we really looked forward to seeing this particular form of mediumship. Jean and I had never actually seen it demonstrated, although we had read and heard how it worked. A psychic artist not only gives clairvoyance as Jean demonstrates it, but at the same time draws a portrait of the communicating spirit for you to keep.

On the evening in question the medium's first contact was with Joan, a friend of ours who was sitting next to Jean and myself. He began by giving Joan a description of a woman that could have applied to anyone's grandmother. During the clairvoyance the medium was drawing on a large sketchpad. I whispered to Joan that maybe he wasn't a natural clairaudient and had difficulty hearing the message from spirit, but as he was obviously clairvoyant to be able to draw the spirit he could see, she should get a good likeness of her grandmother. When the medium had finished with Joan, she was asked to come to the front of the church and collect her drawing.

Joan walked down the church to the platform and the medium handed her the drawing. As she came back she was shaking her head and holding her mouth with her hand. When Joan returned to her seat she said she couldn't believe it. I thought she meant that the likeness was so good she couldn't believe it, until she passed us the drawing. The so-called psychic drawing of Joan's grandmother was nothing more than a giant-sized 'matchstick lady' with a large hat on. Surely this must be some sort of joke. The medium went to other people giving very ambiguous evidence and presenting them with his 'drawings'.

After the demonstration had finished the man left the platform and went into the little tearoom at the back of the church. At Dawley church the mediums often enjoyed a cup of tea after their services, talking to the members and exchanging views or elaborating on messages they may have given during the service. I hurried into the little room as soon as it was polite to do so, only to find that the 'medium' had left at once. All the drawings that people had received were either a matchstick man or a matchstick lady: the only way you could tell the difference was that the ladies had hats on. It was as well the man had left quickly as there was no sympathy for his performance. Muriel, who had booked this so-called psychic artist, still recoils with embarrassment whenever I remind her of our first experience of psychic art.

Another medium who holds a special place in our hearts from that particular time was Mr Connibere. We remember him well for his total honesty and his unique presentation. No one, including himself, would call him a brilliant medium, but we often recommended other people to see him if possible. If you were feeling a bit down or fed up, an evening with Mr Connibere was guaranteed to make you feel better.

When he appeared at our local church it was always full. He would begin his demonstration by saying how surprised he was to see so many people in the church. 'I can only assume that you have nothing better to do, or that there is nothing very good on the television tonight. Still, I'm glad to see so many because I will need all the help I can get, for I'm not that good. But I guarantee we will enjoy ourselves.' In all fairness there were times when he was brilliant, and this was usually followed by a quip such as 'That was very good, wasn't it? I wonder what happened?' If he was having trouble getting a member of the congregation to accept the evidence, he would stop and say to the person, 'You really haven't a clue about what I'm saying, have you?' When they apologised, saying they hadn't, he would usually reply, 'That makes two of us. What do you suggest we do now?' He would look towards Muriel and ask if the kettle was on yet for tea.

We both admired him for his honesty. When he was good he was very good, but when he was bad he admitted it, and his professional presentation got him out of trouble. He never once tried to hoodwink or cheat the audience and he was respected for that. Some years ago we heard that he had taken a position as a resident medium in a hotel in Devon. We wish him all success, knowing that he is bringing pleasure to a lot of people and working for spirit in his own particular way.

We were fortunate and privileged to become a good friend of Mr Gordon Higginson, who trained Jean and helped her a great deal when she began her development. Anyone involved in spiritualism will probably have heard of Gordon as he has been the president of the Spiritualist National Union for many years. He is a 'materialisation' medium as well as a brilliant clairvoyant. We attended a course of lectures Gordon gave in Birmingham, and after a series of talks covering most forms of mediumship, he said he would try to demonstrate the most remarkable form of mediumship that can ever be witnessed, materialisation.*

There were probably about fifty people who had attended all the lectures, and Gordon only agreed to demonstrate his remarkable gift to us at the final lecture, when he was sure that everyone knew what to expect and there was no danger to himself. This form of mediumship is the most hazardous for the medium, who is put into a very deep trance state indeed, and any sudden disturbance can have disastrous effects.

When we arrived for the demonstration all the men were given cloakroom tickets on entering the hall. A woman was picked from the audience and asked to select two tickets from the bag. The two men whose numbers were chosen were asked to go into the small room and search Gordon completely and then hold his hands and lead him on to the platform. At no time during the whole of the evening did the two men let go of Gordon's hands. Before the demonstration began the two men standing on the platform holding his hands said they had searched Gordon *completely*, and emphasised that they meant completely, and had then watched him get dressed. They said that Gordon was wearing a pair of briefs, trousers, an open-necked shirt and a pair of sandals, and that they had searched the clothes before passing them to him. They were entirely satisfied that he could not have hidden any other materials on his person.

We were told beforehand that we must keep the same seats that we had occupied during the lectures. Jean and I and the friends we had gone with for the lectures happened to be sitting in the front row. We were only a few feet from Gordon so we could see clearly everything that was happening. I must stress at this point, and I know Gordon will forgive me, that as this was my first experience of this phenomenon and I still had a

* A full explanation of materialisation is given in *More To Life Than This*.

sceptical attitude, I was purposely looking for any kind of deception.

The lights were turned down on a dimmer switch but there was still enough light even for those sitting at the back of the hall to see. We watched as Gordon was put into a deep trance by his friends in spirit, very quietly and without any heavy breathing or shaking. Cuckoo is a little girl who works with Gordon from spirit, as Lucy works with Jean. Cuckoo asked one of the men holding Gordon's hands to unbutton his shirt. We all sat on the edge of our seats waiting for something to happen. Slowly we noticed ectoplasm begin to emerge from Gordon from the solar plexus region of his body. At the same time we noticed it coming from his nostrils. The ectoplasm from the solar plexus and the nostrils linked together and flowed over his lap on to the floor. It was only inches from my feet, and Cuckoo must have been reading my thoughts, for she said that those near to the ectoplasm could touch it but it must be treated with great care. Jean and I both bent over and reacted in the same way by snatching our hands away at once after touching it. It was freezing cold. The hall had been closed up, and fifty people sitting packed together made it very hot indeed. The only way I can describe ectoplasm is that it is like the thick foam from a fire extinguisher. When I bent down again and looked at it closely, I saw that it was vibrating, and I can only say that it seemed *alive*.

Paddy, another of Gordon's friends from spirit, then said that they would try to materialise a little girl who was waiting to show herself. The ectoplasm began to form into a shape. We could see two little feet forming and then two little legs, and the beginning of a skirt of some kind taking shape. It became obvious that the little girl was sitting on Gordon's lap. We could see that she had crossed her legs and one leg was swinging back and forth. The spirit was half-formed when suddenly Paddy announced that owing to the very hot atmosphere they felt it was too much of a strain on Gordon and that they would have to end the materialisation. You could hear the groans of disappointment round the hall. The form of the little girl began to break down and the ectoplasm started to return to Gordon's body. A large piece of ectoplasm detached itself from the main body and was at our feet. Jean and I and three other friends sitting close to us watched in fascination. Suddenly it simply disappeared like a mass of washing-up liquid bubbles and there was nothing there.

Paddy said that to make up for the obvious disappointment that spirit felt from the audience they would treat us to another form of mediumship, 'apports'. He called a woman's name from the audience and asked if she would come up to the front of the hall. Paddy said that her father wanted to communicate. He had planted a rose tree in his garden just before his very quick and unexpected passing to spirit. Paddy said that he wanted to give his daughter a present and would she please do as Paddy asked. She agreed.

Paddy asked if she would turn to the audience and roll up the sleeves of the blouse she was wearing. The woman did this and opened both of her hands to show that she had nothing in either. Again, we were only feet away from the woman. Paddy then asked if she would mind placing one hand into the small amount of ectoplasm still on Gordon's stomach. She said she couldn't, until Paddy reminded her it was her father's request that she did as he asked. Slowly we saw her place her hand into the ectoplasm and after only a second or so she snatched her hand away and screamed. We could see protruding from the ectoplasm what appeared to be a rose. Paddy again asked if the woman would carefully take out what had been apported. Slowly she took out a beautiful, perfect yellow rose. She began to cry and between tears explained that her father had planted a yellow rose tree. She handed the rose to us in the front row; it was a lovely rose stem with thorns and there was even dew on the flower. The ectoplasm returned completely and eventually Gordon came back to normal consciousness and asked if the seance had been successful.

If you have never experienced this form of mediumship I

can understand that your first impression on reading the last few pages might be 'What a load of rubbish. I don't believe any of it.' I can only say in all honesty that what I have just described actually happened. I was deliberately looking out for any form of fraud or trickery, and I stake my reputation when I say that there was no fraud of any kind that could possibly have taken place. However, I can still understand people who say that they would have to see this with their own eyes before they could believe that such a thing is possible.

This form of mediumship is the ultimate in evidence that we and spirit have yet achieved. The amount of patience and training that is required by a physical medium to achieve this type of mediumship is one reason that materialisation mediums are so rare. If ever you have the opportunity to see it demonstrated, don't hesitate. I can assure you that it is not at all frightening and is, to say the least, fascinating.

It is precisely to protect the good name of mediumship that when Jean hears or reads of anyone showing disrespect towards spirit, or of a medium upsetting people, she takes steps to stop this despicable behaviour. A woman who recently came to see Jean proved once again the importance of choosing one's medium with great care.

I received a telephone call from the woman asking if it was correct that my wife was a medium. I replied that this was so. Her next question came as a refreshing surprise. 'Your wife is a genuine medium and not a fortune teller? I don't want the services of a fortune teller. I need the help of a genuine medium.' I confirmed that Jean was a qualified medium with certificates to prove this, and she made an appointment for herself and her husband. We call this a 'double sitting': Jean will often see two people together if the couple are closely related.

The reason I say it was a refreshing surprise when the woman asked if Jean was a genuine medium is that many times on answering the telephone I hear the question: 'Is that the home of the clairvoyant?' From the tone of voice and the manner in which they ask, I can tell that they are seeking the services of a fortune teller. When I explain that Jean is a 'clairvoyant medium' they are often taken aback and some reply, 'Does that mean she talks to dead people?' I no longer take the time to explain exactly what Jean's work for spirit entails but simply say, 'Yes, she does.' The reply is usually that they thought Jean 'read the cards or the palms or that sort of thing'. Normally these types of enquiry do not result in an appointment.

I can understand why some people are confused as to what exactly Jean does, because of the word 'clairvoyant'. Many fortune tellers use this title to describe their type of work, and they are right as far as describing their ability to see into the future. It must be stressed that *some* fortune tellers do have a remarkable gift and seem able to predict future events for people. In the context of Jean's work, however, the word 'clairvoyant' means her ability 'to see spirit'.

When the woman and her husband arrived for their appointment, I showed them as usual into the kitchen. Having checked that Jean was ready to receive them, I took them through to the sitting room and closed the door before returning to the kitchen. Jean had no more sittings booked for that night, which was to prove a blessing. In the very short time I had spent with the couple I had the distinct impression of reticence and caution from them and felt that Jean was in for a very difficult sitting. My feelings were soon to be proved totally unfounded.

After about an hour I heard the door open and was surprised to see Jean come into the kitchen on her own. She asked me if I would make some coffee for everyone and join them in the sitting room. I took the coffee into the room and waited to find out what had happened. Jean said she wanted me to listen to the recorded sitting (the couple had obviously agreed), and to hear the recent experience the couple had been subjected to. The recorder was switched on and Jean's voice could be heard testing that the recorder was working correctly. It may be of interest to mention that Jean always tests the recorder before commencing the sitting, for a very interesting phenomenon has

93

on occasions taken place. After the sitting has finished and the recorder is played back, Jean's voice can be heard clearly during the psychometry, but when she hands the object back to the sitter and then commences to link with spirit and pass on any communication, the recording stops. There is often just a noise that sounds like very strong atmospheric interference and no voices at all can be heard. When Jean closes the sitting and begins to sum up what has taken place, her voice can be heard again clearly and distinctly. We can only assume that, for reasons known only to spirit, they have chosen not to allow a recording of their communication to take place. On this occasion spirit had no reason to block the recording and this was the tragic story I heard.

Spirit had immediately made their presence known to Jean as the couple entered the room, so there was no need for her to ask for an object to hold for psychometry. Jean described a young man who had actually walked into the room with the couple. She said the young man had sat down next to them and had told her he was their son. I will not dwell on the tragic details of their son's death as I don't wish to cause those concerned any further distress, but he had died from the result of smoking in bed and setting the bedclothes on fire. His parents were obviously devastated by this, and friends had been unable to console them in their grief. It had been suggested by a friend that maybe a medium might be able to offer them some consolation. The couple had never had any experience of this sort of thing and were understandably sceptical. Eventually, however, they had decided that they would seek the help of a medium in the hope of being given the comfort of knowing that their son was now out of danger and happy.

Having, as I said, no experience of mediumship, they chose to visit a lady who advertised her services in their local paper. What took place on their visit is unforgivable when one considers the emotional state they were in following their son's tragic accident. Thank God they had the fortitude to continue their search and eventually find Jean.

On this first encounter with a so-called medium, they were seated at a table while the woman took out a pack of playing cards. She began to spread the cards and then started to tell the couple about their probable future. Quickly they explained that this was not the reason for their visit. The 'medium' seemed quite put out by this statement, and when the couple explained that they had come to try to receive some kind of communication from a loved one who had passed, she was very shocked. 'I don't get involved in that sort of thing. Did you know it can kill you? Who was it you hoped to contact?' she asked. The couple told their sad story, to which the woman replied, 'Well, you have lost him now. If they don't communicate in the first few weeks, then they can't communicate after. The best advice I can give you is to leave the house because it must be full of bad vibrations.'

I could now understand the telephone call asking if Jean was a genuine medium, and also the reticent attitude when the couple arrived. We spent the rest of the evening explaining that Jean had received communication from spirit friends within hours of their passing and also from spirit that have been in the spirit world for years. As time is not relevant to spirit, their communication is not governed by how long they have been in the spirit world.

The couple asked if moving house would affect the closeness of their son that Jean had affirmed to them. Jean explained that their son was close to *them*, not to the location. Wherever they chose to live, their son would remain close. After a long discussion the couple were just about to leave when Jean smiled and said, 'He's still very close to you. He's just said he will be with you in September.' They said that September was the month of their son's birthday. Jean said that they should buy him a card for his birthday. They thanked Jean for the help and comfort that she had given them and said how relieved and happy they were to know that their son too was happy and safe. Jean repeated once more that they should totally ignore the nonsense that the other woman had told them, and promised to take steps to see that she did not upset any other people.

We wrote to this woman and explained that she had no right to advertise as a medium as she obviously had no idea of how a genuine medium works or of the sort of help they can offer people. We politely advised her not to pass comments on a subject that she had no knowledge about. We were pleased to hear at a later date that she had changed her title to 'fortune teller and psychic'. At least now people who made appointments with her would know what they could expect to receive.

This example, although it had a happy ending, demonstrates how careful one should be in choosing the right sort of person who can offer the help you require. If you seek the services of a medium, always check first that it is a genuine medium you are going to see and not a psychic or a fortune teller. Check that the medium is qualified, and if possible only go on the recommendation of someone you can trust. If you are not sure, ask questions when you make your appointment and ask if you can take a tape recorder. If the medium is genuine, he or she will have nothing to hide and should be happy for you to record the sitting. In this way you will avoid making a mistake which could be very upsetting and could have serious consequences.

Chapter Eight

Strange Encounters

Jean has a very active interest in the Tudors. I have often said that our house could be compared to the Tudor room at the National Portrait Gallery. We have pictures of Tudors everywhere, and over the years Jean has collected ornaments with Tudor connections. She has a library full of books on the Tudor period and has become quite an authority on the subject. Most of our holidays are taken in areas where there are strong Tudor ties, either Tudor buildings or places lived in or visited by Henry VIII.

Hever Castle in Kent is Jean's favourite place to visit. It was the home of Anne Boleyn, where Henry did much of his courting of Anne. On our first visit to Hever, Jean had a very strange experience. She had by this time developed her sensitivity and found on many occasions that she was able to 'pick up' feelings and atmospheres from historic houses we had visited. She had no previous knowledge of the castle except that it was Anne's home.

When we arrived we parked the car and walked to the castle entrance. Hever is in a truly magnificent setting, with very spacious gardens and surrounded by a moat. We stood admiring the castle and then crossed the drawbridge before entering a large room that was used as the reception area. It was a beautiful wood-panelled room with a staircase leading from one corner. I saw a guide seated by the entrance and was about to walk over to her when I noticed Jean standing in the centre of the room with a puzzled look on her face.

'What's the matter, love?' I asked.

'It's all wrong. This is not how it used to be,' Jean said, still frowning. 'This used to be the kitchen. This was where all the food was prepared for the house. I can sense people cooking and there was a long scrubbed table in the middle. I can see large fires and ovens and all the utensils hanging from hooks. It looked nothing like it does today.' I inspected the large room but there was no indication whatsoever that it had been used for the purposes Jean had just described.

The guide who had been seated at the door must have seen us looking bewildered and came over to us. She smiled and said, 'Excuse me, can I help you? You seemed to be looking for something.' I explained that Jean was a medium and how she had felt the room was not at all as it used to be. The guide asked if we had visited Hever before. I said this was our first visit and we knew nothing about the history of the building except its association with Anne Boleyn. The guide said she noticed we hadn't bought a guide book yet and led us over to her desk. She took a guide book from the pile and turned to a page that confirmed everything Jean had just described. The room we were standing in was indeed the kitchen in Tudor times, and was known as 'The Great Kitchen'.

The guide was fascinated with Jean's ability and asked if we would return to her desk after our tour so that Jean could share any further 'feelings' she might experience. During our tour Jean told me she had a very strong feeling of Henry and Anne in one particular bay window in the long gallery. When we returned to the guide she confirmed once again that this was correct and that Henry and Anne had spent many happy hours together in the long gallery. The woman asked Jean what her general feeling had been about Hever. Jean said it was hard to put into words how she felt. 'It's a feeling of coming home. I feel happy and safe. The castle seems to wrap itself around me. Does that sound silly?'

The guide said that Anne had spent some of her happiest years at Hever. 'You don't think you could be Anne reincarnated, do you?'

We laughed and Jean said, 'Not at all. I think I have simply sensed the happy atmosphere retained in the castle.' We have been back to Hever several times since that first visit. Jean has never seen or experienced anything out of the ordinary, but always comments on the happy atmosphere combined with her feeling of returning home.

Another time we were on a visit to Warwick Castle when suddenly Jean said she heard a woman's voice telling her that there was a particular picture she should look for in the castle. Jean described how the woman in the picture was dressed and what headdress and jewellery she was wearing. We looked everywhere but could not find any picture resembling the one Jean had described. We tried a second time, still in vain. Jean stopped and sat down for a few minutes, and closed her eyes while I waited. Suddenly she stood up and said she knew exactly where we should go. When I asked how, Jean smiled and announced matter-of-factly: 'Easy, I just asked my friend.' She then led me to a room with lots of pictures round the walls. She walked deliberately to a particular spot and pointed to a small portrait hanging high on the wall. It was difficult to see the detail but it was of a lady dressed as Jean had described. We could not make out the writing on the picture, so we asked a guide if he knew whose portrait it was. The man said it was not a good likeness but it was a picture by an unknown artist of Anne Boleyn.

Jean has once actually even been in communication with Anne Boleyn. We had been sitting for half an hour in one of our development groups on a Monday evening. Jean mentioned that a woman had drawn close to her. Joan, who had been sitting with us for over a year and whose integrity and total honesty were unquestionable, also became aware of the same woman. Joan told me that the woman was dressed in a beautiful Tudor dress, and Jean said that she had told them her name was Anne. I immediately became suspicious and defensive. In such cases I am always very wary that the imagination of the person being used as the channel for communication with famous people may have been allowed to influence the medium's mind. This time, however, 'Anne' began to talk to us about the attitude towards famous people in the spirit world. She emphasised that no matter what high position or status people may hold in this physical world, it does not influence their position or afford any special favours in the spirit world. She spoke of the levelling experience death has on us: we all enter this world in exactly the same manner, naked and vulnerable, and we leave it taking the only possession we came with – our spirit.

She spoke of her home, Hever Castle, and gave various names of servants and other people employed at the castle during her life there. Eventually I said that, knowing of Jean's interest in the Tudors and the many books she had read on the subject, it was difficult for me to accept without reservation that the woman was who she was purporting to be. The response was quick and positive: 'I care not, sir, what you think. Look to Lambeth for your proof.' And with that statement she left.

We discussed the communication afterwards and I still voiced my scepticism strongly. I had assumed that the name Lambeth referred to a person, but Jean couldn't think of such a person linked in any way to Anne Boleyn. Some years later Jean was reading a book and asked me to read a particular chapter. It was about the divorce that Henry VIII had sought from Katherine. It stated that meetings between Archbishop Cranmer and Anne to discuss the prospects of the divorce were held in secret in the vaults of Lambeth Palace. Jean swore to me that until she had read about it in this book she had no idea of the link between Lambeth Palace and Anne. Only recently has she read that Elizabeth Boleyn is believed to be buried at

Lambeth. Even this does not prove to me beyond doubt that we have spoken with Anne Boleyn.

Brian had been sitting in the group for some years and, like Joan, his integrity was unquestionable. One evening he became aware of a famous personality who had made his presence known to him. Brian said he felt it was the spirit of T. E. Lawrence (Lawrence of Arabia). It is a well known fact that Lawrence was very interested in spiritual matters. Lawrence began by talking of his campaigns in Arabia and, although most of this information is readily obtainable, my suspicious nature again came to the fore. There were times when for short periods Lawrence spoke in what we could only assume was Arabic, as the language was unfamiliar to anyone present at the time. He spoke of a dagger that had been given to him by a Bedouin tribesman whose life he had saved in the desert wars. He said the dagger could be found above the fireplace in his home, Clouds Hill. When Jean and I were on holiday in Dorset we made a special visit to Lawrence's home only to discover that much of his personal belongings had been taken to a small museum nearby in Wareham. We found the museum and included in the items is a dagger given to Lawrence by a Bedouin tribesman.

Because of my suspicious nature I asked during the communication if there was any significance in his speaking to us at this particular time. It was Monday, 12 May 1975, and he told us to check the date against his life story. We discovered that T. E. Lawrence passed to spirit on 13 May 1935. Brian said he had no special interest in the life of Lawrence, and most certainly did not know the date of his death. We had no cause to disbelieve him.

Certainly Jack Benny was very upset when he spoke to us, as he said it was one of the rare occasions he had given a performance without the possibility of receiving a fee! And Jack Hawkins the actor gave us a very moving address on the world being a stage, and we merely players in the production of life.

There have been other famous people we have received communications from, including Maurice Chevalier, Louis Armstrong, Jane Seymour and Bing Crosby. It would be wonderful to say that over the years these and many other stars have spoken with us, but I stress in all sincerity that no such claim can be made without speculation and reserve.

There is always a great danger of allowing your imagination to distort your judgement and encourage false assessments of the presence of spirit. We were particularly reminded of this when we recently visited one of the most famous places associated with hauntings and psychic phenomena, Borley rectory and church. Jean, Andrew and myself were on holiday staying in a village a few miles from Borley. We had planned to visit the church – the rectory was burned to the ground following a prediction said to have been received from spirit, and the hauntings were reputed to have been transferred to the church. Various psychic investigators had stayed in the church for long periods with their tape recorders, monitors and other complicated sensors, and claimed to have recorded strange noises and spirit presences. It was with an air of expectancy that we approached the church.

The day was lovely and sunny as we parked the car and walked up the tidy path leading to the church entrance. We commented on the beautifully kept churchyard and proceeded into the church. Our first impression was of a quiet ordinary country church; there were no exceptional monuments or anything else that made it stand out from any other small village church. Jean and I both adopted the attitude we have learnt from experience is important when we are asked to investigate psychic disturbances: we push what we have been told, or in Borley's case what we had read, to the back of our mind. I felt quite at ease as we went our separate ways looking at the monuments and various dedications on the windows to local dignitaries.

Jean had chosen to sit quietly on her own in one of the pews. After some time Andrew and I returned to Jean and asked if she had sensed or received anything at all from the atmosphere in the church. Jean said she felt only a peaceful and tranquil atmosphere and nothing even resembling the frightening events others said they had witnessed. We must have spent half an hour in the church, and during the whole time Jean said she felt happy and never once uncomfortable or threatened. We left the church and returned to the car.

It had been a very interesting visit all the same because it showed how important it is not to let other people influence your own perceptions by their experiences. Ironically, however, spirit did make their presence known to us in a most positive way during our week's visit to Essex.

The cottage we were staying in for our holiday was a converted out-house of the old farm. Soon after our arrival we had all heard strange noises coming from different parts of the cottage, such as footsteps and doors opening. Sometimes only one of us would hear the noises, and when we asked the others they had heard nothing. There were times when the three of us heard the noises simultaneously. We had all at different times asked each other if we had visited the bathroom during the night, because of the sound of footsteps. The answer was always no.

When we first walked into the cottage Jean said at once that there was a spirit presence there. Andrew and I had not taken much notice of Jean's statement, for we had become somewhat resigned to her ability to sense the presence of spirit. But because of the obvious presence that we all heard, we asked Jean who it was. She said it was a man. She had tried to communicate but he was either not aware of our presence or did not wish to speak to her. Jean said she felt he was a farm worker who was still close to his place of work, and that he seemed quite happy.

During the week our friend made his presence known on several occasions. One night Jean and Andrew had gone to bed before me. I had stayed up to watch a particular television programme. When I finally went to bed I noticed that Andrew had left some books on the table. The books were closed and stacked on top of each other. Before I went to sleep I heard the now familiar footsteps coming up the hallway. I woke Jean and we both heard the sitting-room door open. As we lay listening, we could both hear the pages of books being turned. Slowly and very quietly we went and opened the sitting-room door. The cottage was all on one floor and our bedroom was next to the sitting room. As we opened the sitting-room door, the noises stopped at once. The books were spread over the table and two of them were opened. I told Jean that only a short while before I had seen the books neatly stacked and all of them were closed. Jean smiled and said, 'How lovely. He was probably just curious and was thumbing through Andrew's books. When he was working on the farm he probably couldn't read, for in those days many people never had any sort of education. He was simply fascinated by the books.' When we left the cottage we all made a specific point of saying goodbye to our friend and wishing him a continued happy life.

Chapter Nine

Down to Earth

One of the most important motives for writing my books is to show that despite Jean's gift we remain very normal, down-to-earth people. Of course our way of life has changed since Jean has developed her gift, but we as people remain the same. To demonstrate our way of life today, the following is an account of a typical week in our lives. It will show how hectic and demanding the life of a medium can be. But, more important, I hope it will reveal how common sense is the guiding principle of our work.

SUNDAY: Service at Bloxwich Church 6.30 pm.

We allow ourselves a bit of a lie-in this morning; we get up at about 10.30 am and have coffee and toast. Jean begins the normal housework while I check the car and clean it in readiness for the service tonight. I then begin preparing the lunch. This is often interrupted by telephone calls from churches where mediums who are booked are unable to take the service, and we are asked if we can take their place. Today I explain that we are already committed. We have lunch at about 1pm. After lunch we settle down to watch the omnibus edition of our favourite programme, 'EastEnders'. Get a bit annoyed as the telephone rings half-way through; it is someone wishing to book a private sitting.

3 pm. I tell Jean that I am going into the kitchen to begin my preparation for the address I have to give tonight. I put my special music tape on and try to tune in to my friends in the spirit world. Eventually thoughts begin to filter through. 'Yes, that sounds interesting, Chi (my special friend from spirit), we spoke about that some time ago. I think that theme will go down very well tonight.' I feel a little better now that I know what we will be talking about tonight. I walk up and down the kitchen formulating and building the skeleton of our address until it is fixed in my mind. I thank my friends and then go into the sitting room to tell Jean we have the address for the night. 'Good. I wish I could prepare the messages beforehand like you,' Jean says, looking worried. She has been very quiet all day. I know how she has been thinking about the service tonight and talking silently to her friends all day, hoping that it will be good. I say that it is nearly 4 pm and I will run the bath.

Since the end of 'EastEnders', Jean has been engrossed in one of her Letter Fit puzzle books. For years Jean has bought this type of puzzle book each week, as they help her to switch off from the worry and thought of a demonstration. I call down that the bath is ready. 'Oh well, here we go,' Jean sighs as she begins her preparation for the evening service. I know from experience that casual conversation has now come to an end. I also have a bath and then put on my suit and return to the kitchen. I put my tape on again and refresh my memory of the address. I feel the inspiration coming through again and am aware of the presence of my friends. I send out thoughts to Henry and Lucy, asking them to be near to Jean and help her with her work tonight.

5.15 pm. Jean comes down dressed and ready to leave. 'How do you feel?' I ask.

'All right,' Jean replies with that familiar anxious look on her face.

We set off for the church. It's a terrible night, freezing cold and with the rain pouring down. We park the car outside the church and Jean puts her last tape on the machine. As we sit in the car, we can see the people arriving for the service. 'There's going to be a good crowd tonight, love,' I say quietly.

'Oh God, I wish there was some way I could get rid of this feeling.'

'Do you feel rough?'

'Terrible. Look at all the people coming. Please, Henry, let it be good, please!'

The final track comes through clear on the cassette player in the car. It has always been the last song Jean listens to before any demonstration. The words have a very deep meaning for her and complete her preparation. It is from the Neil Diamond cassette *The Jazz Singer*, and the song is entitled, 'Hello, My Friend, Hello'.

We entered the church, and the service had only just begun when suddenly I noticed an old shaggy dog enter the Church. He shook himself, and the rain sprayed off him in all directions. He slowly walked down the aisle and then lay down by the people in the front row. A member of the church got up to lead him away, but I stood up and asked if anyone knew whom he belonged to. No one knew, so the man began to lead him away. I said to leave him where he was as he was obviously a stray, and it was still pouring down outside. He lay down again and the service continued. When we began to sing the first hymn he sat up and joined in. He yowled and whined as we sang, and as we sang louder so did he. After the hymn there were smiles all round as he sat down with everyone else. The hymn before the address he again joined in with all his strength. When I stood up to speak he looked at me and then fell asleep. When I finished the address I said I was pleased to see that only one member of the congregation had found my address so boring that he had fallen asleep.

When the service had ended I made sure the dog received his tea and biscuits the same as everyone else. A man said he would take him home with him and try to find his owner. It was a lovely experience for us and I'm sure our friend enjoyed the service and his refreshment afterwards. I don't think he would have been too disappointed that he didn't receive a message. At our next visit to Bloxwich Church we enquired about the dog, and were told that the man who took him home was unable to trace his owner. He decided to keep the dog himself. It was a lovely gesture by him and I feel that spirit may have had something to do with it.

The service went very well and the address and Jean's demonstration were well received. Following our cup of coffee and a talk with some of the congregation afterwards we set off on our journey home. As always we talk about the service and criticise or compliment each other on our work. On arriving home we both go and change immediately into casual clothes. Jean always changes into her nightdress and dressing gown and thanks her friends for their help. 'Well, we didn't do too badly, did we?' is a common remark from Jean.

I prepare some supper for us both as we are always starving hungry after a service. Jean settles down in the sitting room and switches on the television. We have supper and try to unwind by watching the television. There is a late-night horror film, *Salem's Lot* about vampires and the undead. We were enjoying the film and having a few laughs at the special effects, which I'm sure some people would find very frightening. I had mentioned to Jean that it wouldn't surprise me to receive a telephone call from someone saying they were experiencing trouble with spirit in their home. It is not uncommon if a particularly frightening film is being shown on television for us to receive a call asking for our help to clear a house of a spirit presence.

It was past midnight when the telephone rang. I got up and smiled at Jean. 'Here we go. I told you, didn't I?' I was surprised to hear Muriel's voice. 'Bob, I'm sorry to phone so late but I've just had a call from some young girls who are afraid to stay in their cottage.' Having known Muriel and Bill for twenty years, we knew that they were not easily taken in by people's imagination. Muriel explained that she knew the mother of one of the girls, and she had mentioned to Muriel some time ago that her daughter and friend had been experiencing some form of psychic disturbances in the cottage. The girls had not been too bothered by this, but the disturbances had recently become quite frightening and the girls were now very alarmed. I said that we would be ready and Muriel said she would be up at our house in a matter of minutes. I passed on Muriel's message and Jean went straight upstairs and got herself ready to go out. Muriel and Bill arrived and we set off on the twenty-odd-mile journey. Fortunately Bill knew where the cottage was, so it was no problem finding it in the dark. Jean as usual sat quietly, preparing herself for what might be expected of her when we arrived.

The cottage was part of a stud farm and it was obvious from its construction that it was very old. The two girls introduced themselves. They were very agitated, and their two boyfriends were also frightened even though they tried to give the impression they weren't. They all verified the phenomena that had been taking place in the cottage over the past few months.

The girls said it had begun with a feeling that they were being watched. This feeling grew stronger, and then they noticed that things in the cottage were being moved around. At first they had accused each other of moving the items, until they proved that someone else was responsible. They then began to notice a strong smell of alcohol. Whenever anything strange happened it was always accompanied by the smell of alcohol. In recent weeks the girls and their boyfriends had all heard someone moving about the cottage and the sound of voices. The most positive evidence of the presence of spirit, however, had come with the interference to electrical appliances: kettles were switched off, lights and the television were switched off and on. I immediately asked if the electrical circuits had been checked and was told that a qualified electrician had examined the cottage and found nothing wrong.

More a Way of Life

That evening they had been watching television and the set had been switched off and on continuously. They had all heard the sound of voices and footsteps, and eventually they telephoned Muriel. (The girl's mother who knew Muriel had given her daughter Muriel's number in case they needed it.) While the young people explained what had been happening, Jean had gone on her usual 'walkabout' by herself. When she came back to the room she nodded to us, indicating that she was aware of spirit's presence. The television had been left on but with the sound turned down. At the precise moment Jean came into the room the set switched itself off. The very next instant it came on again, and we all noticed the strong smell of alcohol in the room.

I explained to the four young people that Jean would now try to communicate with whoever was responsible for the disturbances. I stressed that nothing dramatic or frightening was about to take place, but that Jean would simply talk to spirit and the rest of us would hear nothing and probably see nothing. Jean told us that as she walked round the cottage she had seen two men and a lady – she had the feeling they were a family. She then settled down in a chair and closed her eyes. The rest of us continued talking among ourselves quietly. The girls were asking questions about our work and wanted to know why spirit should try to frighten people. I said that in our experience spirit did not deliberately try to frighten anyone, but simply wanted to attract attention to their presence.

Jean eventually opened her eyes and smiled with a look of satisfaction. 'You won't be troubled any more; my friends will be taking care of the family. It's a very sad story. The younger man I saw told me his name was Tom. He lived with his parents in this cottage years ago. His father was a leading hand on the farm and this used to be a tied cottage. I noticed that Tom's father walked with a crutch, and Tom told me he had lost his foot in an accident on the farm. Tom had taken over his father's duties so that they could keep their home, but his father had become very bitter and had taken to drink.' This was the reason for the smell of alcohol in the house. The father's anger and bitterness had kept the family bound to the cottage and prevented them progressing in the spirit world. Jean said Henry and Lucy and her other friends would take care of the family and help them on their spiritual pathway. Jean said Tom apologised for his father's behaviour and had mentioned that the family were buried in the local churchyard.

The girls said they had heard something about the history of the cottage from the owners of the farm, and could remember reference to Tom's family. They said they would try to find out more about the family now they were satisfied that the disturbances were not of an evil nature. Jean reassured them that they would have no more trouble from spirit. She said she always feels concerned for spirit in these circumstances, and thanked the girls for giving her the opportunity to help spirit. She asked them to telephone at once should they ever feel or think that spirit were still in the cottage. Muriel kept contact with the girl's mother, and we hear that they have never experienced any phenomena since the night Jean spoke to Tom.

We finally collapse into bed at 2 am.

MONDAY: Four private sittings booked, start 12.30 pm.

We get up about 8.30 am and have our toast and coffee. The postman arrives with a pile of letters: most are for Jean asking about private sittings, or describing people's experiences and asking what should they do about them. Jean puts the letters that need replies into her folder. She does the normal household chores and takes over the job of answering the telephone as I lock myself away upstairs to get on with writing this book.

11 am. I come down and make us both a cup of coffee. Jean goes upstairs and begins her preparation for the sittings. I set out the cups and books and so on for the sitters, and when everything is ready I return to my little room to carry on with my writing. At about 12.15 pm Jean settles down in the sitting room to await the first sitter. I listen for the doorbell, welcome the sitters and take them in to Jean, and after the introductions

the sittings begin. Today they are all individual sitters, so I have to keep an ear for the doorbell as I carry on with the book.

One of the sitters today is a woman with a foreign-sounding name. Jean told her that her husband had walked into the room with her. The communication was instant and very short: 'Tell my wife not to blame herself for my passing. Tell her I have found my mother and my father and my brother. We are all together and will be near to her all the time until we are all reunited in spirit.' Jean said that her husband had gone and no one had taken his place from spirit. The woman was very emotional and said that she needed no more evidence that it had been her husband communicating.

The husband was Polish and during the war he and his family had been taken to a German labour camp. His wife explained that her husband had seen his father die in the camp and his body tossed out to be eaten by wolves. His mother had been separated from them and he had never heard from her since. His brother had somehow escaped from the camp and nothing was known about him. The woman said that her husband had spent years trying to find his brother and had returned to Poland many times making fruitless enquiries. She now knew that he had been reunited with his family and his search had ended. She had blamed herself for his death because she was a very good cook, and felt that she had overfed her husband and that that may have been a contributing factor to the unexpected heart attack from which he had died. Jean was able to reassure the woman that she was in no way responsible for his passing. She then apologised for what had been a very short sitting, but the woman said that she needed to hear nothing more and was delighted that her husband was now at peace.

Usually at around 4 pm Jean has finished the sittings and looks very tired. I decide to finish my writing and help her get the evening meal ready. She changes into her tracksuit and we eat at about 5.30 pm. We have a bath at about 6 pm and look forward to a quiet night in front of the television. Jean picks up one of her puzzle books and tells me she is not at home if anyone rings. Immediately the telephone rings; someone wants to talk to Jean. I explain that she is busy and ask if I can help. It is an enquiry about a discussion group: 'Can we come and talk to their group?' I look in Jean's diary and offer a few dates. The telephone rings regularly throughout the evening for sittings. I make the appointments and Jean copies them into her own diary. By 10 pm Jean is very tired and goes to bed. I say I will be up later. I am one of those lucky people who need only a few hours' sleep; I rarely go to bed before midnight, and often get up in the early hours and read through what I have written the day before. Because of my sleeping habits I often sleep in Wendy's old room so that Jean can have an undisturbed night's sleep. She has always needed plenty of sleep, and if we have a late night it takes her a couple of days to get back to feeling normal again.

TUESDAY: We never book sittings for Tuesday, as this is the day Jean does the shopping and washing or catches up with her baking. But today at about teatime the door bell rang, and on opening the door I saw a woman standing in the porch. I asked if I could help her. 'I'm not sure that I've got the right address. Is this where the "medieval" lady lives?' she asked.

Not sure that I had heard her correctly, I apologised.

'My friend said she thought this was where the medieval lady lived, and I would like to see her.'

Trying to conceal my laughter, I explained that Jean was a medium, not medieval. Still very serious, the lady asked what was the difference. I replied that Jean as a medium was able to receive messages from loved ones whom people had lost and pass these on to relatives and friends. The woman's face lit up and she turned to her friend who was standing at the bottom of the path. 'You were right, Doris, it is the right house and it sounds as if she will be able to help me.'

Feeling a little embarrassed as she shouted to her friend I

asked if she would like to step inside and make an appointment.

She leaned forward and began to whisper, 'I don't want to say too much but, you see, my husband walked out on me some years ago and I've lost all contact with him. He said he was just popping down to the shops and I never saw him again. You say your wife gets messages from people who've been lost, so I'll get in touch and come to see her.' With that she turned round and headed off down the path to her friend Doris who was waiting for her. They walked away chatting happily.

I stood there laughing to myself and shaking my head. She hadn't given me a chance to explain that I hadn't meant *lost* in the context she had used. I closed the door and went into the sitting room to explain to Jean what had happened. I repeated word for word what had happened and we both collapsed with laughter. We felt sorry for her for having lost her husband in such a way, but it amused us that she thought Jean could receive a message from him. Jean added that, although we were both getting older, to describe her as medieval was a bit over the top.

Later on the telephone rings. It is a man who says his name is Wayne from Beacon Radio, a popular independent local radio station based in Wolverhampton. He presents a Sunday-evening live programme called 'Wayne's Speak Easy'. He would like Jean and myself to come along to the studio next Sunday at 9.45 pm to talk about my book and Jean's life as a medium. The programme goes out live between 10 and 11 pm and Wayne explains that there will be people phoning in with comments or questions. I say that this will be no problem and we look forward to meeting him next Sunday.

In the afternoon I get a telephone call asking if I can visit a house to give a man healing. As we have nothing planned for this evening I arrange to be there at 8 pm. I leave Jean in the middle of washing and baking, and arrive home again at about 10 pm. Jean asks how the healing went and I explain that it will involve a long regular treatment and that I have made appointments to see the man every Tuesday night for as long as it takes.

WEDNESDAY: Four sittings starting at 12.30 pm.

The same morning routine as before – Jean doing the house-work, me busy writing. The sitters arrive; this time they all come together, so I can relax and have a good session of writing without too many interruptions. Jean doesn't finish her sittings until about 5 pm. One sitting went on much longer than normal, and I ask her why. Apparently at the end of the sitting Jean asked the woman if she had any questions. She replied that she had enjoyed the sitting but was surprised that the answer to the very serious problem which had brought her to Jean had not been mentioned. Jean said that she also was surprised, as spirit usually offer help or advice in these circumstances. She asked the woman if she would like to tell her what the problem was. 'I'm pregnant and my husband is not the father.' Jean replied that she had other sitters in a similar predicament and that spirit friends usually offered some advice or help during the sitting. The woman then said that her circumstances were probably different from the others. 'You see, my dear, *I'm pregnant by spirit*.' Jean apologised, thinking she had not heard correctly. 'I have been visited by spirit for many years now,' the woman continued, 'and my friend from spirit made love to me and I am pregnant.'

Never having faced this situation before, Jean was quite taken aback. Tactfully she tried to explain that it is impossible for anyone to become pregnant as the result of spirit. The woman would not accept this, however, and Jean as politely and quickly as possible got rid of the woman, saying there was nothing she could do to help. When Jean broke her normal rule and told me about the sitting, I said: 'Well, I thought you were as close to spirit as it's possible to get, but she could certainly teach you a thing or two.' I added that she would have a unique case if it led to a divorce, and Jean said she would have to have a word with Henry and make sure he didn't get any funny ideas. We had to joke about the incident because we found it impossible to take it seriously.

THURSDAY: One sitting 1 pm; discussion group 8 pm

Jean gets up looking tired. She hasn't had a good night and is more concerned than usual about the sitting today. The woman is travelling all the way from Glasgow to see her, which is why Jean has only booked one sitting for today. She is always conscious of the fact that her mediumship can never be guaranteed, and this anxiety becomes greater when she knows that people are travelling huge distances to see her. I try to be extra helpful by doing the chores and giving Jean as quiet a morning as possible.

At mid-morning I suggest a nice hot bath in the hope that it may relax her a little. Jean lies down for an hour and falls asleep. I wake her gently at about noon and she gets ready. She still looks nervous and I try to comfort her, saying I am sure that Henry and Lucy won't let her down. Jean says she knows that, but she's worried that she may let *them* down. I say she can only do her best: no one can expect any more than that.

1.10 pm. The woman arrives, having set off at 5 am to be sure of being punctual. The sitting lasts for an hour and a half, and Jean spends another hour talking to the woman and advising her on her problems. I join them with coffee and learn how well the sitting has gone. The woman says it was worth the long journey, for Jean has helped her enormously and given her the strength to 'go on living'. It's nearly 5 pm when she leaves, after asking Jean and me to sign her copy of my book she has brought with her. We wish her a safe journey home and Jean closes the door with a sigh of relief. I say, 'Well done, love. Now sit down and relax because we've got a discussion group tonight.' The television goes on and I smile as the puzzle book comes out of the cupboard.

The meeting tonight is at a Young Farmers group near Newport. Jean says she is pleased it's not too far to drive, and asks me to make sure we leave at a reasonable hour. We make the usual preparations and arrive at 7.45 pm. The meeting goes very well and the questions keep coming long after the agreed time for the meeting to be finished. Jean is hyped up and she and her spirit friends are working well. She is bombarded with young people handing her objects to psychometrise and is doing her best to accommodate as many as possible. I am being asked for Jean's business cards by people who want to make private appointments to see her. I have to ask them to let us go as Jean is very tired and it is nearly 11 pm. Jean chatters away on the drive home as the adrenalin is flowing fast. She is still switched on, and from past experience I can read the danger signals. Tomorrow she is in for a hell of a day. I decide to myself that I will get up early and take the phone off the hook, and let Jean sleep in for as long as possible. Over the past years I have taken on the role of 'managing' Jean as best I can, which means vetting the amount of work she does wherever possible. This is why she does no planned work on a Friday. Most weekends we have either meetings or services, so I feel it is necessary for her to have Friday off so that she ran recuperate a little in readiness for the weekend commitments.

FRIDAY: No sittings; no meetings

Jean comes down at about 11 am. She has a piece of toast and coffee. She tidies up a little and says she would like to go to Shrewsbury just to get out of the house and have 'a blow'. We go and have a snack in our favourite bistro, Traitors Gate. Veronica, a friend who works in the bistro, is always interested in what is happening in our life and asks how we are. She says Jean looks tired. Jean replies, 'No more than normal.' We have a wander round the shops and eventually arrive home at about 5.30 pm. After a light tea Jean says she must spend the evening answering all the letters that are piling up. I say I will spend the evening writing.

SATURDAY: Workshop at Harborne 3.30 pm; demonstration of clairvoyance 7.30 pm.

We stop on the journey to Harborne, near Birmingham, for a snack lunch as we don't know when we will eat later. We arrive at the venue at 3 pm. There are already quite a few people arriving. We meet the organiser and explain exactly what will happen during the workshop and assessment class. This particular workshop has been organised by the Harborne Healing Centre. The members of the church have been invited along so that Jean and I can assess their mediumistic and other potential.

We are shown into a small room and at our request left alone for about fifteen minutes just before the meeting begins. We have brought our portable cassette player with us and listen to our special music tapes, getting ourselves in the right mood and a receptive state for spirit. Then the president comes in and tells us that they are ready to start. There are about fifty people waiting in the audience as we step up on to the platform.

I begin by talking about the various forms of mediumship and the difference between a psychic demonstration and a demonstration of clairvoyance and clairaudience. I mention that later Jean will be demonstrating both techniques. I explain that this afternoon the audience will be playing a very active part in the proceedings, and that they should not be afraid as Jean and I will be there to offer advice and guidance to those who feel they have the ability. After about half an hour I sit down and Jean stands up to begin the workshop in earnest.

She asks for six volunteers who are at various stages in their development. There is a good response and Jean selects four women and two men. They include some who have been sitting in a development group for about a year, some who have been sitting for a number of years, and two people who have just begun their public demonstrations; one volunteer is a man who has been working on a public platform for nearly forty years.

Jean asks them to come to the front of the hall and form a straight line. She moves into the body of the hall and collects objects from people who have no relationship with any of the volunteers. She then gives a short talk on the subject of psychometry, explaining what you can receive from this form of sensitivity and what you cannot. She makes a point of emphasising that this has nothing to do with spirit. She asks the volunteers to take one object each out of the box. In turn they are asked to psychometrise the object and pass on the information they get to the owners of the objects. The quality and quantity of information given is understandably varied, but after allowing them to try on their own Jean moves along the line and offers suggestions and encouragement. The difference is then quite remarkable.

Jean then announces that the group will switch to clairvoyance and clairaudience. Realising that the group are likely to be nervous she brings out the tape recorder and asks the group to sit quietly and listen to some music. She asks them to link with *their* friends in spirit and to ask for their help in the demonstration. When she is satisfied that enough time has been given for this she asks them all in turn to give a very short demonstration. During this she stands next to each of them, helping and advising with the messages. Once again, the difference in quality and presentation is very noticeable between when they are left on their own and when they work with Jean's help. Following their short demonstration two of the volunteers are separated out. Jean wants to use these two for a special reason. One woman has given a very confident demonstration, speaking to two members of the audience. Jean did not interrupt her and she sat down looking very pleased. Jean now asks the woman to stand up again, and then she turns to the audience. 'What is the most important objective a medium must strive for, and what is the sole object of clairvoyance and clairaudience?' The answer comes positively and clearly from the audience: 'To prove survival of the spirit after physical death.' Jean turns to the woman, who looks embarrassed. 'Where was spirit in your demonstration, my love, and who was communicating to the people you spoke to?' she asks.

'I don't know,' the lady replies.

Jean then explains that what we have witnessed is a marvellous demonstration by a psychic, but not by a medium. The woman has given people a great deal of information about themselves, what they have done, where they have been and whom they have met, but there was not a single fact about spirit. Everyone agrees with Jean's appraisal, although some of the audience admit that they hadn't realised the messages the woman gave were not from spirit. Jean tells the woman not to feel bad. 'You are a very good psychic, but as yet you haven't channelled your sensitivity towards spirit. With the proper training you may very well become a good medium.' Jean asks for a round of applause for an excellent psychic demonstration, and the woman returns to her seat looking pleased.

The other volunteer Jean has singled out is the man who has been working for nearly forty years. 'Please excuse me, but I have to say to you that over the years you have fallen into a bad habit and one that is very common on our platforms.' I could sense Jean's reluctance to criticise someone who had been working in public almost twice as long as she had. The man is very understanding and says he will welcome any advice Jean has to offer, and we can sense he means it.

'When you were demonstrating,' Jean explains, 'you gave each person you were talking to a lot of names from spirit. You asked if the people could accept them. When they said they couldn't accept some of them, you said, "Well, take them with you, they will mean something later." It is *your* responsibility to clarify the identity of the names. If someone you are talking to cannot accept a name of a person from spirit, then you hand it back to your friends in spirit. I say something like, "Henry, I need more clarification and information. *Get it*." You must only ever leave a name or person from spirit with the recipient if after very exhaustive searching and questioning by you and your spirit friends you can get no more information. Normally in these circumstances I leave the person and promise to come back to him later in the demonstration. I send a thought to Henry to get his finger out and damn well deal with this problem. Almost without exception, by the time my demonstration has ended I have returned to the person with more evidence that clarifies the doubt.'

Jean speaks at length on the importance of being honest with the medium. 'If you cannot accept a message, then say so. Don't feel sorry for the mediums. If they are competent to be on a platform, they should be good enough to clear up any messages that are not understood.' This draws a spontaneous round of applause from the audience. The man says that Jean is right, and in all the years he has been working this is the first time another medium has offered such advice and guidance.

We then open the meeting to questions and answers. This continues until the president says we have run out of time. There are groans and a quick discussion takes place. It is decided that, if we agree, the meeting can continue for another half-hour. I choose two volunteers who have just begun taking the platform as 'inspired speakers'. I give them each a subject to talk on and a few minutes to collect their thoughts. They both make very good short addresses and I simply give them a few suggestions on improving their presentation. For example, one gave his address with his eyes closed, and when I ask why he says that he felt the inspiration flowed better and it helped his nerves as he couldn't see the audience. I say I can understand the second reason but not the first. I suggest that the next time he is asked to speak he keeps his eyes open, and he will be surprised at the confidence he gets from noticing when members of the audience agree with what he is saying. I added that he can always avert his eyes from those who have fallen asleep or are shaking their heads.

Eventually the time runs out and we close the meeting. There is a lovely buffet tea provided by the ladies of the church. Jean and I are allowed to sit quietly in the little room on our own, although a few people come in to ask questions and see if we will come along at a future date. We say we would love to.

Jean has about half an hour to prepare for her evening demonstration of clairvoyance. When we come out on the platform the audience has doubled, a normal situation. Jean begins by saying that she had better give a good demonstration as there are a lot of people present who were at the workshop. She mentions that she will demonstrate what she spoke about in the afternoon, and that she has given away a few secrets. The demonstration goes very well and there are plenty of people who come up after saying how much they have enjoyed the day. We arrive home at about 10.30 pm.

SUNDAY: Evening service at Hall Green, Birmingham 6.30 pm; Beacon Radio 10 pm.

A bit of a lie-in this morning, then breakfast, prepare lunch, answer telephone for sittings, etc. In the afternoon I begin preparation for my address this evening. We set off for the service at about 5 pm. It goes very well and we manage to leave the church by about 8.30 pm. We drive back to Wolverhampton and arrive at Beacon Radio by 9.30 pm.

Jean and I are sitting in reception waiting to meet Wayne when there is a knock on the door. Jean says jokingly: 'I bet it's the local vicar who has been invited along to put the other point of view.' (Wayne has said nothing to us about anyone else appearing on the programme.) I open the door and a man walks in. 'Hello. You are Robert, aren't you, and this must be Jean. I'm Roger Hinton, the vicar from Bushberry near Wolverhampton. We are on the programme together, I believe.' Jean and I smile at each other as we shake hands, and I think to myself: Wayne, you crafty old devil, you probably thought we wouldn't come if we knew a vicar was coming too. He needn't have worried, as Jean and I have discussed our way of life with several clergymen over the past years.

A young man called Mel comes down to take us through to the studio. There we meet Wayne, who sits us round a table with microphones attached to it. We are given headphones for the calls that may come in from the public. It is 10 pm and Wayne introduces Roger, Jean and myself. He talks to Jean about mediumship and then asks Roger for the attitude of the

Church towards mediumship. A general debate follows. Roger's main point is that he feels mediumship is unnecessary. We stress that Jean is booked up months in advance for private sittings and that spiritualist churches are filling every week with new faces, many of whom are Christians dissatisfied with orthodox doctrine and philosophy. Many people are finding spiritualism and mediumship *very* necessary. I say that obviously many people attending other churches affiliated to other religions are satisfied and happy in their own way of life and may find mediumship unnecessary, and we are pleased for them.

Roger asks if we consider ourselves Christians? I say that we are spiritualists, but as we both believe in Jesus Christ, his life and his example to us all, I feel that qualifies us to call ourselves Christians. Roger then brings the Apostles' Creed and the crucifixion into the discussion, asking our opinion on these. I answer by saying that as spiritualists we accept our own personal responsibility for our actions and thoughts and how they affect us and others. We cannot accept that our sins can be automatically forgiven and erased because of the crucifixion of Jesus. I add that spiritualism does not demand the reciting of any creed or obedience to any dogma, but is open to interpretation and understanding of the seven principles of life on which it is founded.

We hear that many people are waiting to phone in. During the hour-long programme I begin to feel a little sorry for Roger, as the majority of calls are praising Jean for her work and saying how much spiritualism has helped them. One caller (as expected) quotes the chapter in the Bible saying that it is a sin to work as a medium. We answer that any religion can find quotations in the Bible to complement its beliefs and condemn those of other persuasions. There are many documented examples of the mediumship of Jesus himself, so the quoting of biblical verses to strengthen a biased attitude is in my opinion worthless.

The programme finishes at 11 pm. Mel comes into the studio

123

and asks if Jean and I will pop into the studio next door. We meet another presenter who has taken over the broadcasts but who wants to talk to us before we leave. He is fascinated by Jean's work and we spend another half-hour talking about it to him. We then accompany Wayne and Mel into another room and are eventually joined by three other people from Beacon Radio. We sit talking until nearly 1.30 am, with Mel booking a private sitting and Wayne saying he would love to have us back again to cover more aspects of mediumship on another programme. We arrive home at about 2 am.

MONDAY: Four private sittings, first at 6.30 pm.

Another week is under way, and I wonder what surprises it has in store for us. I know that with spirit's help we shall survive.

Chapter Ten

A Special Year

Our way of life has changed again recently. It was coming up to the Christmas of 1986 and Jean was aware that something was in the air. I had been asking her for more details of this feeling she had had, but she couldn't get a clarification from spirit. She said that the only answer she got from Henry when she asked was 'Be patient, all will be revealed in the near future. I am very busy, but you are right: there is a dramatic change coming into your life, a change that we have been planning for a long time. I have told you many times that you only receive from spirit what you have earned. Recognition for anyone's work only comes after years of devotion and hard work. We feel you have earned this recognition, so be patient. Soon you will see what our plan is for you and Bob.'

Neither Jean nor I could understand this message. We could only carry on with our work for spirit and, as Henry had asked, be patient. I too had had the feeling that 1987 would be a very special year in our lives; for one thing it was the year we would celebrate our silver wedding anniversary.

When my first book was finished I had submitted the manuscript to several small specialist publishers who had replied with very favourable reports but had not accepted it for publication. In January 1987, following the advice of a friend, I had written for the first time to one of the publishing giants telling them of my book. I received a reply from Tom Weldon, an editor at Macmillan, asking me to send the manuscript. I posted it, and as usual got on with other business and pushed any thoughts of acceptance out of my mind.

I had not told Jean that I had submitted my manuscript to Macmillan. In a very short time compared to the other publishers' responses, I received a telephone call from Tom. Jean answered the phone and called to me, 'There's a man on the phone from Macmillan wanting to speak to you. I haven't a clue who he is or what he wants.' Tom said he had read my manuscript and felt that there was a very good chance that Macmillan would publish the book. My reaction on putting the phone down caused Jean some concern as I danced round the room like someone demented. When I had calmed down I explained that Tom was coming from London the following week to meet us and discuss my book. Jean was as delighted as I when she realised what this news meant to both of us.

On the day of Tom's visit I was like a child on his first day at school, excited yet very nervous. We were due to meet an editor from one of the largest publishers in Britain to discuss the possibility of publishing my first book. I had arranged that we would meet Tom at the station and then go to lunch at our local pub. I put on my best suit and Jean wore her best Laura Ashley dress and had her hair done specially. Then we set off to meet Tom.

Having no knowledge of publishing or the people working in this field, I had formed a picture in my mind that an editor from such a prestigious publisher as Macmillan would be middle-aged and rather serious, the image of the typical London businessman. I had described myself to Tom on the phone so that he would recognise me, and said it was unlikely that there would be many 'ginger-haired, bearded and rather portly men' waiting at the small station at Telford. As the people left the London train I looked for someone resembling the image I had formed. Two men came towards me carrying briefcases and dressed in smart suits. I smiled and made a move towards them. They smiled back and walked straight past, probably thinking to themselves what a strange character I was. Suddenly I felt a tap on my shoulder. 'Mr Cull? Hello, I'm Tom Weldon. Pleased to meet you.'

As I turned to see who had spoken to me my image of the editor from Macmillan was shattered. I was talking to a young man of about twenty-five, dressed in very casual clothes and carrying a plastic shopping-bag. We set off to lunch and spent a wonderful day discussing the book and its publication. From the first moment of our meeting we got on really well together, and Jean, Tom and myself have become the very best of friends. As Tom was leaving to return to London, Jean said that the name Jack should mean something to Tom. She said it was not the name of a relative but he would soon recognise it. Soon after we had a letter from Tom saying how delighted he was to be publishing my book, and adding that the name Jack was indeed significant, for on returning to London he realised that Jean had given him the title of a book he was publishing, the biography of C. S. Lewis. Tom added that if Jean was in touch with Lewis, could she tell him that only that week a decision had been made to delay publication of his book, and it was hoped he wouldn't be too angry. Jean replied jokingly that she had passed the message on, and that Lewis was not angry at the delay in publication but he was a little worried as to how Macmillan would get his royalties to him in the spirit world.

When the excitement of the news about my book settled down, I said to Jean that I *knew* 1987 was going to be a special year and what a wonderful start this had been.

In March we celebrated our silver wedding. We wanted to invite all our close friends and, as our house was too small to hold them, our two friends Beryl and Grenfell kindly opened their lovely cottage to us for the day. We asked Eric Hatton, a very good friend and a spiritualist minister, to conduct a reblessing of our marriage which he did with great sincerity and reverence. It was a wonderful day and another treasured memory of our 'special year'.

Tom had suggested that some pictures of Jean and me working in public would be interesting for my book. So it was arranged that a photographer called Marcus should come the weekend we were booked to take a service at Stourbridge Church, where Eric Hatton is president. As Marcus was returning to London immediately after the service, he followed us to the church in his own car. When we parked in the church car-park Marcus said that Tom wanted a picture of Jean sitting in a car, as there were references in the book to her ability to assess the road-worthiness of other people's cars. Marcus suggested that Jean should pose for the photograph sitting in his car. You will see in the book a picture of Jean sitting holding the steering wheel of Marcus's car. What the picture does not show is the worry on Jean's face as she got out of the car. 'You've got a serious problem to do with the steering of your car,' Jean told Marcus as she got out. Marcus smiled and said, 'You are joking, aren't you?' Jean, who was hyped up ready to begin her work for spirit, said that she was very serious and had picked up a definite defect in the steering linkage. She suggested that Marcus get it looked at as soon as possible.

Marcus was now looking concerned. He admitted that the steering had felt 'different' on his journey up from London. He asked Jean if she felt it was safe for him to drive back to London that night after the service. Jean said that, although she felt it was important to get the problem seen to as quickly as possible, she did not think Marcus would be in danger by driving back to London. We heard from Marcus after he had arrived home safely. He took his car in for a check and the mechanic found that the steering links to the front wheels were very badly corroded and worn. He said it was as well that the car had been brought in, adding that if the car had been driven on very rough roads or the steering wheel had been pulled sharply a serious accident might have occurred. Jean said she felt it was not a coincidence that Marcus had suggested she sat in his car for the photograph. He said that if he ever bought another second-hand car he would try to get Jean to sit in it first.

We were invited by Macmillan to attend a sales conference so that Jean and I could meet the reps who would be selling the book to the bookshops after publication. Laura, who had been assigned as our publicist, booked us into a posh London hotel for our stay. When we arrived we both felt very intimidated by the atmosphere of this exclusive hotel. We took most of our meals in our room as we felt nervous about going down to the restaurant. On one occasion we ordered coffee in our room. As we were pouring the coffee we found that the cream had gone off. Jean telephoned room service and we were brought fresh cream and more coffee. When the waiter came into the room he realised that he should have brought clean cups. He was very apologetic and said he would fetch some more. Jean said it didn't matter as she could wash up the cups we had in the bathroom. The look on the waiter's face and his reaction were priceless. 'Madam will do no such thing,' he said. 'I will bring you fresh cups and saucers.' I'm sure it must have been the first time in his life that a guest had suggested such a thing and it probably caused a good laugh in the staff quarters afterwards.

Whenever we ordered food it was always accompanied by fresh fruit. There was always far more than we could eat. Jean asked what happened to the food that was not eaten, and was told that it would be thrown away. From then on all the fresh fruit we didn't eat was placed in the small fridge in our room. When we got the train back to Telford after our stay, Jean was carrying a shopping-bag full of lovely fresh fruit. We didn't buy any fruit at home for a fortnight.

Jean was asked if she would give a short demonstration for the Macmillan sales force. The conference was booked at the Oaklands Park Hotel in Weybridge. It had been arranged that a driver would collect us from our London hotel and take us to Oaklands. Jean was very worried about the demonstration, as she felt that the success of the book depended upon it to some degree.

The car arrived at the arranged time and we set off on the journey to Weybridge. Gordon the driver was a super person, and he and I chatted away about Jean's work as a medium while Jean as usual sat quietly preparing herself for her important demonstration. Gordon was saying that although he was sceptical about the subject he found it fascinating, but had had no personal experience of spirit communication. Suddenly Jean sat up and smiled. 'Gordon, your father is sitting next to you in the front passenger seat.' At that moment, thank goodness, we were travelling along a wide stretch of road, for Gordon turned sharply to look at the 'empty' seat and the car veered across the road. Gordon corrected the swerve and said to Jean, 'For God's sake don't do that again.' We all burst out laughing, and Jean proceeded to give Gordon a private sitting during our journey.

Jean said that there had been a strange sort of reunion just before his father's passing. Gordon said that was absolutely correct. The very week before he died, his father had asked Gordon to come home to Glasgow for a special talk. Gordon explained that he had not been very close to his father for some years, and this invitation had taken him quite by surprise. The meeting took place and Gordon felt that his father was trying to strengthen their relationship, as if he knew something was about to happen. The following week his father suffered a massive heart attack, from which he passed. Jean said that his father was now trying to apologise for the distance that he had put between them, and that he was feeling guilty as the division had been his fault. Jean went on to give more personal details about Gordon's father and Gordon himself. Suddenly Gordon pulled over to the side of the road, and after regaining his normal composure – this had been an emotional experience for him – smiled and announced that we were completely lost. He said he had been listening so intently to Jean's message that he had not concentrated on his driving. He said why should he worry: 'I'm driving a clairvoyant, so which way should we go, Jean?' We all fell about the car as Jean replied, 'I haven't got a bloody clue. Do you think your dad would know the way?'

Eventually Gordon realised we had simply missed the exit road and turned round and drove back to the right exit. Gordon said Jean should not worry about the demonstration she was due to conduct, as she must be well tuned in to have given him such a marvellous message. Jean said she too felt more confident now.

We drove up to the front of the magnificent hotel, and Jean and I got out of the car and walked up to the entrance. We had been told to ask for Laura when we arrived. Two very smartly dressed gentlemen were standing by the doors leading into the hotel. We asked them if it was possible to tell Laura that we had arrived. Their reply was simple and to the point: 'NO.' We walked away and Jean said, 'Charming . . . I hope they are not the sort of people I'm expected to demonstrate to or it's going to be a difficult time.'

A woman came over to us and asked if she could help. We explained the circumstances and she said she would fetch Laura. When we told Laura how helpful the two men had been she smiled and said, 'It's no wonder; they are two of the bodyguards for the Duchess of York.' We had forgotten Tom had told us that Macmillan were promoting on the same day a book edited by the Duchess of York.

After we had waited for a few minutes a host of people came into the reception area accompanied by the Duchess of York. We were asked if we would like to meet Fergie but Jean said she was too nervous about her demonstration and would probably only make a fool of herself. There was a wonderful buffet laid out and we were invited to help ourselves to anything we liked. We explained that we could never eat anything before a demonstration, but that afterwards we would be able to do justice to such a spread. Tom and Laura had mentioned that there would be about twenty or so reps present at the meeting, so it wouldn't be too overwhelming for us. I had been asked to speak for a time on the book, followed by a short demonstration from Jean.

Eventually the Duchess of York left and everyone returned to the conference room. Laura sat with us as we waited for the cue that they were ready for us. Jean had got up and walked to the window and stood by herself looking out at the gardens. Laura looked worried for Jean and asked if she was all right. I explained that Jean was just moving into top gear of her preparation and was best left alone. Tom came out and said that everyone was ready. Without a word between us we followed Tom into the room, and the sight that greeted us was a shock. Rather than the twenty or so people we had expected, there must have been at least fifty seated all round the room. One table included most of the top directors of Macmillan plus a full complement of the reps.

I stood up and gave a short talk on the writing of the book and its content and then, knowing it was Jean whom everyone was looking forward to meeting, I introduced her. Jean came out to the middle of the room and as usual without a sign of nerves said that in the very short time she had she would demonstrate the difference between Jean the psychic and Jean the medium.

Jean walked up to the directors' table and asked Martin for his watch. She walked back to the centre of the room and began to tell the man about his house move, the condition of his health and other personal details. He agreed with everything Jean said, and I could see many heads nodding in agreement as the facts would be known by his colleagues. Jean handed the watch back, saying that was psychometry, purely psychic and nothing to do with spirit communication. 'Now I will show you how mediumship works.'

Jean spun round and said she wanted to speak to a gentleman seated half-way down one side of the room. 'I have a man here who has a brother named George. You know George and this man wants you to tell George that he has arrived safe and well. The man I'm talking to won't give me his name but he tells me he has only just passed to spirit.' The reaction from the man receiving the message was incredible. He held his head in his hands and muttered, 'My God.' He became very emotional, and despite the fact he was sitting with his colleagues and bosses, unashamedly let loose his emotion. Jean gave some more details but quickly cut the communication short to save the man further embarrassment. Jean moved to another man, giving more evidence of life after death and relatives from spirit. Tom leaned over and asked me if I would tell Jean to finish her demonstration. I said to Tom that it was not necessary for me to tell Jean to finish. Henry would be aware that Tom had asked Jean to end, and would tell her accordingly. When Jean had finished with the second man she turned to everyone and said that she had been told that her demonstration must end, and then thanked them all for their co-operation in making the demonstration so successful. As we rose to leave the room there was a spontaneous round of applause for Jean.

We left the room with Tom and went to the lounge for a drink. The buffet had by this time been cleared away, and as usual we were starving as we hadn't eaten a thing that day. Tom was very apologetic, but we told him not to worry as we had been in this situation countless times. It was arranged that Jean and I should spend some time talking personally to the reps after the formal meeting. When the meeting closed two men came to our table and asked Jean if she would have a word with John (the first man Jean had communicated with) as he was still very upset about his message. Jean went off and continued talking to John in private about the communication he had received from spirit.

I was surrounded by reps all eager to hear more about the book and Jean's work as a medium. One rep asked why it had taken me so long to accept Jean's mediumship as being genuine. He said that he himself had been very sceptical before Jean's demonstration, but that in a quarter of an hour she had totally convinced him of her ability. He said he was a personal friend of John's and had been amazed by the message. He had also attended the funeral of George's brother only a few days previously and knew how upset George had been about the passing of his brother. He said that Jean could not possibly have known anything at all about the circumstances of his death. Jean spent another hour giving short private sittings to groups of people until it was time to return to London. We drove back with Gordon, who said how pleased he was that it had all gone so well. It really was a memorable day for all concerned.

Following publication Jean and I were invited to radio stations for chat shows, national papers wanted articles and the whole media have shown interest. It came as a particular surprise when the telephone rang one day and a man introduced himself as the editor of 'Kilroy', the BBC television programme. He had read my book and asked if Jean and I would like to appear on the programme they were planning on mediumship and reincarnation. I said we would be pleased to come along provided that Jean had enough warning so that she could rearrange her sittings and so on. The man said that it was still in the planning stage and he would notify us in due course.

Some time later we received a telephone call on a Tuesday asking if we could be at the Lime Grove studios that Thursday. Jean always does private sittings on Thursdays, but she phoned the sitters who had booked for that day and asked if they could come on the Friday instead. Fortunately all of them could change their appointments, so we accepted the invitation.

We were just about to leave the house when the telephone rang. It was the editor of 'Kilroy', saying that after discussion they had decided to do two separate programmes. They had realised that mediumship and reincarnation were two different subjects and warranted individual coverage. They had chosen the subject of reincarnation first, but we were still welcome to take part. The editor explained that we would not be guest speakers this time, but it would be good experience to come along to the studio and see how the programme was run. He said they would be doing a programme on mediumship at a later date.

The programme was scheduled to be recorded at 3.30 pm. The train was due at Euston at 2.40 pm, giving us ample time to get to the studios. Because of a points failure or something the train actually arrived at 3.15 pm. When we got a taxi and explained that we had to be at Lime Grove by 3.30 pm the taxi driver said we might just about make it. I have never had such an exhilarating journey in my life (well, that's one way of describing it). Jean was a nervous wreck when we arrived at 3.29 pm exactly. 'We did it, didn't we?' was the contented remark from the driver as I paid the fare with shaking hands.

On entering the studio we were given tickets with our seat numbers on them. We were taken to what was called the hospitality room where tea and coffee were available. When we had had our coffee and recovered from the taxi ride we noticed some familiar faces. There were some of our spiritualist friends, and because the programme was on the subject of reincarnation some hypnotherapists had been invited. Among them was Joe Keeton, a hypnotherapist who had 'regressed' Jean some years earlier.

Regression is the experience of taking a person back through their life under hypnosis until they are asked to go back before they were born. A very startling phenomenon sometimes occurs at this stage. The person under hypnosis suddenly begins to relate to an entirely different personality. He or she can give uncannily accurate details about the life of this stranger: where he lived, how he lived, how he died, details of locations and places associated with his life, and so on.

We had invited Joe Keeton to our development group some years previously. Jean and I thought it would be interesting for the group to learn how other individuals expand the ability of the human mind other than through mediumship. We discussed with Joe our work in the group and his interest in regression. It was arranged that the group should visit his home in Liverpool and he would try to regress some of the group.

When we arrived at Joe's home he tested each member to find who was the most susceptible to hypnosis. He said that

Jean was an ideal subject and would try regression with her. First he put Jean into a very deep hypnotic state and asked her to go back to various ages in her life. Jean responded by talking about some of the experiences she had had at the different ages Joe took her back to. Eventually he asked her to go back to a time before this life.

Jean suddenly began to talk in a very different accent. She said her name was George Roper, and following a very intensive questioning session using old maps and reference books the following story unfolded. Jean said she was George, who earned a living as a thief and pick-pocket in London in the latter part of the eighteenth century. She gave street names and buildings that were checked out against the maps and books. George eventually married, and from the proceeds of his illegal activities opened a shop selling pies and other home-baked products. Most of the information George gave us about the cost of the ingredients used in his baking, Joe verified from his substantial collection of books from and about that period. Joe asked Jean many questions relating to the time George said he was living in London, which I knew Jean could have no knowledge of.

In my opinion regression does not prove reincarnation, for the facts that are given about another personality could be from various sources and stored in the subconscious mind of the person under hypnosis. It has been suggested that the information could even be memories inherited from our ancestors. As we inherit looks and personalities from our parents and grandparents, we could also inherit some of their memories. Regression and reincarnation are both subjects open to speculation and question but, like mediumship, I think they are fascinating.

After talking to Joe and other friends we were led into the recording studio for the programme. The studio was divided into three banks of chairs, and we soon realised that those who were sympathetic towards reincarnation were seated together, those against were seated opposite, and those who hadn't made up their minds were in between. As the programme got under way it became very heated and we could see why the various sections had been separated. Jean and I enjoyed listening to other people's experiences and the comments of those who dismissed the whole subject as rubbish. It reminded us of the many discussion groups we have led on mediumship, and the reaction of the total sceptics.

When the programme had finished we were again taken to the hospitality room where we spent a fascinating time exchanging views with representatives from other religions. First we got involved with three marvellous people, a Hindu, a Buddhist and a Sikh. They asked what religion we were, and when I said we were spiritualists they were very interested in our replies to their questions. Did we believe in God and in Jesus? I explained that we believed in a divine power that is present in all living things, and accepted all people as brothers and sisters from our Father God. We see Jesus as an example to us all; we accept his teachings but adapt them to a more scientific and questioning age. I also explained that Jesus was a very gifted medium and examples of his mediumship and healing are well documented in the Bible. They replied that their religions have many similarities with our philosophy, especially on the progression of the spirit after death. I stressed that the main difference between spiritualism and the major religions of the world was the aspect of communication from the spirit world. I was pleased when they said that they accepted the fact of spirit communication provided it was executed with responsibility and respect. It was a wonderful experience sharing our views with people who listened and were not bigoted or indoctrinated against spiritualism. They spoke about their own religious beliefs and convictions, and we all eventually said our farewells in an atmosphere of fellowship and respect for each other's personal religious persuasion. This mutual respect was soon to change as we were approached by other religious representatives.

We found ourselves next involved in conversation with two Baptist ministers, Jehovah's Witnesses and Born Again

Christians. The whole atmosphere was one of hostility towards our belief. Jean made a very quick and polite exit to go and talk to other friends, while I switched into top gear in readiness for the barrage of hostile questions that was imminent. 'You realise that your sort work with the devil?'

I smiled. 'Really? Who told you this? If, when you see the results of spiritual healing and the joy and comfort my wife brings to people who are bereaved, if you say this is the work of the devil all I can say is that he must be a truly reformed character. Mediumship and spiritual healing are practised with the blessing and as a result of the will of God.' Some of them took a step back and crossed themselves for protection against this evil person. I then made a suggestion to each of them. 'I will gladly visit each of your churches and discuss your services with an open and respectful mind, if you will come along to one of the spiritualist services that Jean and I take.' They all gave a look of horror at my suggestion and replied that they would not be allowed to do so by the doctrine of their religion. I then asked what right they had to make such derogatory remarks about spiritualism if they hadn't the first-hand experience of witnessing a spiritualist service, or having a sitting with Jean. Their attitude was simply the result of indoctrination by a very narrow-minded philosophy. I was ready for the next attack that I knew from experience to expect.

'It states very clearly in the Bible that no one should get involved in such things.'

I replied that the Bible can be interpreted according to one's own understanding. I added that it was sad that some people quoted chapter and verse to suit their own beliefs, and used other examples to justify their condemnation of spiritualism. Not wishing to use the Bible for this selfish reason, I suggested they might find the following extracts of interest: Daniel 5:5, Ezekiel 3:14, 1 Corinthians 12: 4–10, Hebrews 1:14, Genesis 15:12, and many others. I said this simply proved that any religion can use the Bible for its own ends, but that it was far more rewarding to see the congregations increasing in spiritualist churches because of the acceptance of our very free and undogmatic philosophy and religious beliefs.

They continued their fruitless exercise in trying to save my lost soul, finishing with that well-worn statement that 'any involvement in spiritualism will send you mad'. I smiled, and looking at my watch said: 'Actually the men in white coats are late in coming to collect my wife and me; you see, they only allowed us out today to come for the programme.' I walked away, as it was impossible to have an intelligent discussion on the difference between our individual beliefs. Although Jean and I never had the opportunity to express our feelings on the programme live, in retrospect the experience was very rewarding and stimulating. We are looking forward to the programme on mediumship. There will obviously be guests who have very strong views for and against and it should result in a lively programme.

As 1987 drew to a close I reminded Jean of my feeling that it was going to be a special year, adding, 'My God, I never realised just how special.' There was still about two weeks to go and I thought nothing could surpass what had already happened, but spirit had kept the biggest surprise of my entire life as the finale to this special year. It was to end with the most wonderful Christmas present spirit could possibly give anyone.

Chapter Eleven

Reunited

In my first book, *More To Life Than This*, I wrote of a communication I received from my natural father through Jean in trance. The chapter was entitled 'Victor', this being the name my father said was given to me before my adoption when I was only a few weeks old. My father apologised for 'giving me away', adding that at the time he had no choice. He gave me his full name, which was Raymond Guise, and said his wife (my mother) was named Sylvia and they had called me Victor. At the time neither Jean nor I had any information about my adoption, and no one else present in the group even knew I had been adopted. My adoptive parents had offered to give me my adoption certificate but I had refused the offer, saying that they had been my parents since I could remember and they always would be. My adoption was only disclosed to me at the age of twenty-two, following a very unpleasant experience for my adoptive father, which I describe in my first book. The communication with my natural father took place many years after the disclosure of my adoption. Shortly after this I asked my adoptive parents for my adoption certificate. The details contained the names of my natural parents exactly as they had been given to me via the communication.

On the publication of my book Tom, my editor from

Macmillan, and Penny who was dealing with the publicity had kindly invited Jean and myself out for a meal in London to celebrate. The book is two stories woven together: how Jean and I were led into the world of mediumship and psychic phenomena as Jean's natural gifts of mediumship were developed, and how my involvement changed my attitude of total scepticism to one of conviction. Even today, however, after all the incredible personal evidence I have received, I still retain this questioning attitude. I now accept the existence and the fact of communication totally, but I continue to look for an alternative explanation before I confidently put the experience down to a spirit source.

During dinner with Tom and Penny, I mentioned to Tom one little niggling worry about the chapter on Victor. I explained that it is a fact that a medium can receive communication from someone still living an earthly life. By the faculty of telepathy a medium can tune in to the thoughts of a living person by accident and pass on their communication. Jean overheard our conversation and was not amused. 'When are you going to accept without question that when I say the communication is from spirit it really is? You should be able to trust by now that I can tell the difference.'

I apologised for the thousandth time but went on to explain my niggling worry. 'Just supposing that the communication I received happened to be through telepathy with my natural father. Now the book is published this information about my natural parents will become public knowledge. It's a million to one chance, but let's just assume my father is still alive and hears about or reads this book. If he contacts me and the media get to hear about it, then surely all the other communications referred to in the book will come under suspicion. It will cast a shadow on all Jean's authentic communications.'

Jean looked at Tom and Penny. 'Good God, what *am* I going to do with him? Now you can see what I have had to put up with for the past twenty years.'

I smiled and apologised once again, adding, 'Well, that's just how I am. How spirit have put up with me for so long God only knows. Still, Lucy still loves me, I know.' We all laughed and Tom said not to worry as he felt the situation would never arise. Jean added that in the short time we had known Tom he seemed to have more faith in her than I had after twenty years of involvement. I bowed my head sheepishly and got on with my dinner, and the subject was never mentioned again.

Just before the book was published *Woman* magazine had bought the exclusive rights to print extracts from it. The article that appeared had a picture of Jean and myself and part of it included the detailed account of my natural father's communication. It gave his name and my mother's name and also my original name.

It was Sunday evening, 29 November 1987. The book had been published for about six weeks, and the demand for sittings had been overwhelming. Jean and I had no service booked that evening so we were enjoying a rare treat of a Sunday evening off. When the telephone rang a man enquired if he was talking to the person whose book had been serialised in the recent copy of *Woman* magazine. I replied that that was correct and assumed that he wished to make an appointment to see Jean for a private sitting. 'Ah good, I had to be absolutely sure I was talking to the right person. You may be interested to hear that my name is Raymond Guise.' I apologised, thinking I hadn't heard him correctly. He repeated, '*My name is Raymond Guise.*'

There was a long pause as the message sank in. 'You say your name is Raymond Guise?' Jean was instantly at my side.

'Yes, that's correct.'

'Oh, bloody hell,' was my spontaneous reply.

The man continued: 'I was given a copy of *Woman* and read the article about your communication with your natural father.' He said he was born in December 1938 and the names mentioned were the names of his parents. It took some moments for the realisation to hit me, and suddenly the anxiety I first felt that I was talking to my father was swept away. If this man was born in December 1938 and I was born in January 1938, then he could not possibly be my father. *I was talking to my brother*. I put this to him.

'Yes, it appears so. I'm sorry if I have given you a shock but I needed to be sure I was talking to the right person before writing to you. After reading the article I phoned a distant aunt, my only living relative (or so I thought), who had been a very close friend of my father before he died.'

'Your father is dead?'

He said his father had died when he was only fifteen years old. 'But you already knew this?'

I smiled to myself and said I was 'just checking'. Jean pointed an accusing finger at me and shook her head. Ray continued that when he telephoned his aunt he asked her if she would be totally honest with him as he had a very important question he wanted her to answer. He asked if there had been any other children in the family besides himself. When she asked why he wanted to know, Ray said that was not important, but it was important that she should tell him the truth. His aunt replied that as there was no one now alive who might be hurt by the information she would tell Ray something about which she had been sworn to secrecy. 'There was another boy born before you but he was offered for adoption immediately after his birth. Your parents gave him the name of Victor.'

Ray said that at this point he used his favourite expression, 'Bloody hell!', which just happens to be mine too. He had not mentioned my original name or said anything to his aunt about what he had read in the magazine. He sent off straight away for a copy of his original birth certificate that stated his father as Raymond Guise and his mother as Sylvia Guise, Ray obviously having been named after our father. Following this proof of mutual parents he had made the telephone call to me. He said that if I would like him to he would send me a copy of his birth certificate and also enclose some photographs. I thanked him for phoning and replaced the receiver, still in a state of shock. Ray had mentioned that he and his family lived in Perth, Scotland.

It is difficult to express exactly how I felt. Jean as usual was far more emotional than I – in fact she began to cry. 'How marvellous to discover after fifty years that you have had a brother all the time.' For me, it still had not registered properly. I had just spoken to a man I had never met or even known existed. He told me he was my brother, and from what he had said there was little doubt that it was true. Yet I felt nothing like I would have expected anyone to feel in similar circumstances. I normally very rarely drink, but I poured myself a large whisky and sat down. Jean immediately telephoned all our friends and told them the fantastic news, but I didn't want to talk about it at the moment.

Over the next few days we both waited anxiously for the postman. On Thursday a package arrived with a Scottish postmark. Inside was a copy of a birth certificate and photographs of Ray and his family. There was also a long letter that read as follows:

Dear Robert,

This is the letter I promised to send you after speaking to you on the phone on Sunday 29th November. I hope I didn't give you too much of a shock. I was unsure whether to write first or phone. The main reason I decided to phone first was to make sure that I was contacting the right person.

As you will see, I have enclosed a photocopy of my birth certificate, it is a copy of a recent full certificate that I sent for to make sure of my Mother's name. Until then I only had a shortened birth certificate which does not give this information, I did know her name was Sylvia but I wanted to be sure before contacting you.

As I told you on the phone, I also contacted a relative in West Bromwich for further information regarding yourself. She confirmed that there was a boy child born to my parents before my birth, and without me saying anything more she said, 'and they called him Victor,' then added that he was adopted. At this point it was *me* who said 'bloody hell'.

At first I thought we were too near in age to be Brothers, when you gave the date of your adoption as March 1938 and my date of birth is December 11th 1938. But the fact that at that date you were six weeks old makes it quite possible. I reckon that your date of birth must be between mid January to mid February 1938 am I right? I think we were both born in the same hospital, maybe your original birth certificate can confirm this. I have enclosed a few photos for you, you can keep the coloured ones if you want to, but please return the black and white one of my Father as I only have a few and I would like to keep them together. Now I will tell you something about myself.

I lived in West Bromwich for about the first twenty years of my life, I understand that Mother left Father when I was about 18 months old so I do not remember her at all. I was in a children's home until Father came out of the army at the end of the war. From then until Father's death when I was about 15 years old, we lived with my Grandfather and his second wife. After my Father died, I stayed on with my Grandparents. Two or three years later my Grandfather died, soon after his death I went into the army (Coldstream Guards) to do my national service, at this time I was nineteen.

During my time in the army I got friendly with a chap from Leeds in Yorkshire. I started writing to a friend of his wife and went to Leeds to meet this girl named Kathy, we were married in 1961.

Before this date in late 1959 I contracted T.B. and was in Hospital for twelve months. I came out of hospital and was medically discharged from the army in 1960.

My wife and I were married in Leeds on the 29th July 1961 and lived there until 1978. During which time our two Daughters were born, Samantha on the 26th Feb 1968, and then Rachel on the 13th Feb 1973. We came to Scotland in July 1978 and have lived in Perth ever since. I work for

'National Standard' as a die-maker, the firm's head office is in Kidderminster and another branch is at Telford. Samantha works at the Bank of Scotland and Rachel attends Perth Academy. My hobbies are mainly rough-shooting and fishing, I do most of my own car and motor cycle maintenance and we enjoy caravan holidays. As you can see from the photos we have a dog she is 6 years old and her name is 'Kerry'.

Well I hope I haven't bored you with all that, I am just trying to tell you a bit about myself and my family.

Hope to hear from you soon,

Yours Ray

As I put the letter down the real emotion came to me. I knew now without a shadow of doubt that I really did have a brother. When we looked at the photographs we saw a quite remarkable likeness. Ray had ginger hair and a full beard, and his hairline was receding exactly like mine. Although he was slightly taller, it was like looking at a photograph of myself. Some days later we took the photographs to our close friends Muriel and Bill. They said they couldn't remember these particular pictures of me, and Muriel was speechless when we told her they were of Ray.

I sent for my original birth certificate that confirmed we did indeed have the same parents. We were both born in Birmingham hospitals. I sent Ray a copy of my birth certificate and photographs of me and the family. I also replied with a long letter that I knew would surprise him with certain similarities he had mentioned in his letter. For the first twenty-four years of my life I had lived in Smethwick, which is only a few miles from West Bromwich. Ray married in 1961, Jean and I were married in 1962. They have two children and so do we, of very similar ages. Ray works at the National Standard in Perth as a tool-maker; I worked for seven years at the National Standard in Telford; I am a tool-maker. I was a very keen fisherman. I have always done my own car maintenance.

We had booked a cottage for Christmas near Windsor. Our son Andrew had just moved to a hotel in Windsor to work, and we felt he would be very lonely at this time of year in a strange place without his friends. We had planned to spend a few days with him and enjoy Christmas together. Two weeks before Ray's telephone call Jean suddenly said she thought we ought to cancel the cottage. I was surprised, to say the least. I explained. that at this late date we would surely lose our deposit on the cottage, and when I asked Jean why she felt this she simply said, 'I don't know, I just have this feeling that we won't be going to Windsor at Christmas.' I tried to persuade her to reconsider it, but from past experience I knew it would be difficult to ignore one of Jean's 'feelings'.

As Ray had given me his date of birth I realised that my letter to him would arrive at about the same time as his birthday. For the first time in my life I went looking for an appropriate birthday card bearing the words 'To my brother'. I enclosed the card in my reply. I said in my letter that we had nothing planned over Christmas (which following Jean's feeling was now true) and suggested that if Ray and his family were free it might be nice to meet up during the Christmas holidays. Ray telephoned me after receiving my letter saying what a super idea, but that we must stay at his home rather than find bed and breakfast as I had suggested. It was arranged that we would drive to Perth on Monday, 28 December and stay until Wednesday the thirtieth.

We telephoned Andrew and told him that we would not be coming to Windsor, but instead were going to Scotland. He was disappointed and curious about the change of plans. We said we were going to see his Uncle Ray. Andrew said he hadn't got an Uncle Ray. I said, 'You have now. I've got a brother!' Andrew was absolutely delighted by the news. He said it was a pity he was so busy over Christmas at the hotel as he would have loved to come with us, but that we must be sure to take lots of photographs and send them to him when we returned.

We set off early on Monday morning for the long trek to

Perth. The journey wasn't helped by the appalling weather: it rained hard all the way. Eventually we arrived in Perth. Ray had sent a map of Perth and indicated where he lived. For most of the journey I had been unusually quiet. It still seemed unreal to me to be driving all this way to meet a brother I had never known and to be staying with a family we had never met. As we drove into the actual road I felt very nervous and all sorts of thoughts were going through my head. What if we are very different in personality? Will we like each other? Will we get on with each other? Will Kathy, Rachel and Samantha like their new relatives? These and many more worries flooded through my mind as we drove up to the bungalow and parked the car.

Jean was first out of the car and I pretended I was looking for something. 'Ring the bell, love,' I said nervously. Jean smiled.

Samantha opened the door. 'Aunty Jean, how lovely to see you!' In a spontaneous gesture she threw her arms around Jean and they hugged each other. I then got out of the car. I put my arm round Samantha and we went into the house. Rachel came into the hall and Jean gave her a hug and a kiss, then Kathy came out and they too hugged and kissed. I was standing at the back feeling very apprehensive. I kissed Kathy and felt her cheeks were wet, which didn't help in trying to keep my own emotions in check. Jean went into the living room first. Ray was standing at the far end of the room with his arms outstretched. Jean went straight to Ray and as Ray held her in his arms she began to cry. Ray and Jean stood for some minutes with Ray patting Jean's head. 'It's all right, my love,' Ray kept repeating. Jean stood back, and then Ray looked straight at me. I was standing in the doorway.

'Hello, my mate, how are you?' I went over. We shook hands firmly and held each other for a moment. I sensed Ray swallow hard as I did the same.

We all sat down and for the next hour or so talked without a pause. Within no time we all said it was as if we had known each other all our lives. We never stopped talking for the whole three days. We all had a lifetime's experiences to share.

During our stay Ray mentioned that he was, or had been, very sceptical on the subject of mediumship. After reading the article about my natural father's communication in *Woman* magazine, Kathy had obtained a copy of my book. One whole evening we spoke of nothing except mediumship. Jean and I answered all sorts of questions from Ray and Kathy and the children. Samantha's boyfriend John was at the house that evening and was especially interested in the subject. Jean was able to sense that he was a very sensitive person and told him that he had some potential as a medium if ever he chose to involve himself further. On our last day Ray said that he would need to rethink his previous attitude towards mediumship. By means of the book and our discussion we had made a chink in his wall of scepticism. I smiled to myself as I compared my brother's attitude to my own; it was a repeat of my experience twenty years ago. I think I would have been a little disappointed if he had accepted all we had said without question. His attitude confirmed the fact that he was my brother.

Ray said one thing in particular that had strengthened *his* conviction that I was his brother was the behaviour of his dog, Kerry. From the moment we arrived Kerry never left my side. When we were sitting talking, Kerry would even sit on the settee and fall asleep with her head on my lap. One morning I took her for a long walk. This was the first time the dog had allowed a stranger to do this; normally she always stayed close to Ray. We all said that she must sense the relationship between me and Ray, and as she felt safe with her master she also felt safe with me.

Soon it was time to say goodbye. It had been a wonderful experience for us all. We arranged that Ray, Kathy, Samantha and Rachel should spend a week with us in Telford at Easter. I now felt a little guilty that I had been so worried as I drove up to Scotland to meet my brother for the first time. We can't wait to meet again.

More a Way of Life

Spirit never use Jean for frivolous reasons. We had assumed that the communication from my natural father had been for the sole purpose of finally changing my sceptical attitude, which indeed it achieved. Now we wonder if there was a double motive. Was it also spirit's intention to reunite two brothers after fifty years apart?

It is 1 February 1988 as I write this. In front of me is a birthday card such as I have never received in my life before. It reads on the front, 'To my brother'.

Epilogue

It is difficult to put into words how the discovery of Jean's latent gift of mediumship and the years that followed this discovery have changed our lives. At first I was worried that Jean was in some way different from other people. Coming as I did from a very religious background, the thought of my wife being a medium filled me with horror.

As the years passed I gradually came to realise that, although Jean was different because of this gift, she was still the same person I had married. She had been born with her gift, and for all the years we had been together before it was disclosed I had accepted Jean as a normal loving person. So why should anything change? Following her development as a medium, Jean did not suddenly behave in any strange way; she remained the wife and mother I loved and respected. Accepting and understanding this hidden aspect of Jean's life took us many years. Throughout this period Jean accepted what was happening as simply an extension of that part of herself she had been aware of since birth. She has often said that nothing has really changed from the days when as a child she saw and spoke to spirit people, although that contact is now clearer and more defined. What has changed is that Jean knows the purpose of it all. This realisation is the major factor that has completely changed our lives.

Many people might say that our life today is not so very different from their own, and they would be correct. I feel, however, that our life now is much more than just 'another way of life'. I believe – and this is my own personal belief, as I know Jean does not share my feelings – that Jean is a very special human being. The gift of mediumship she was born with sets her apart from others. Her life on earth was for the purpose she is fulfilling today. I support and strengthen her will to continue: that is *my* role. Some people achieve their destiny, and Jean is one of them. When you realise this fact your whole attitude to life is changed. All past experiences, even the bad times, take on a totally new meaning, for you know they were leading you to the eventual fulfilment of your destiny.

Many people appear never to ask themselves the questions Why am I here? What is the purpose of my life? The reason for this, I suppose, is that they must be content with their lot. Why is it then that some of these people who are living comfortable lives and are reasonably happy with their circumstances suddenly feel the need to question their existence? I believe it stems from the awakening of an awareness of the 'spirit within'. We begin to accept the finite span of our earthly life, and realise that we all have a reason for living.

Spirit communication is not purely to comfort the bereaved. It is also to prove the existence of the infinite part of ourselves. This knowledge leads to a feeling of responsibility to ourselves and to others. To achieve one's destiny will always result in the service of others.

Today Jean's life and mine are shared with spirit. Jean is a servant, offering her services to anyone in need. Nearly twenty years ago she asked, 'Is there more to life than this?' Her question was answered, and as a result our whole way of life changed. Those of you who have asked the same question, those who seek the truth, those who wish to open new doors, remember a promise that was given to us all: 'Ask, and it shall be given you; seek, and ye shall find; knock, and it will be opened.'

Your Questions Answered

When we are invited by an organisation to talk and demonstrate, we usually follow a format that has proved successful for us over the years. I begin by talking about the many different forms of mediumship and how they operate. I describe how Jean receives communication from the spirit world, and what it is like in the spirit world. I give a brief history of the development of spiritualism, and explain how it is practised today.

Jean then follows my talk with a demonstration of her clairvoyant and clairaudient powers. She shows how she can obtain information by psychometry and talks on the subject of auras. We always leave as much time as possible for questions and answers. This part of the evening has always proved the most popular and is we feel the most important. Once the questions begin to flow, the time limit for the meeting is often ignored. It is usually Jean or I who draws attention to how late it is, and the audience say they had not realised the meeting had gone on for so long. Frequently they say they have many more questions they would like to ask, and want us to return to give them the opportunity to ask these.

There is such a growing interest in the subject and still so many people who do not get the opportunity to air their questions that I feel it would be useful to devote a chapter to the questions that are most often asked, and the answers we have given. I can only include a small selection of the thousands of questions that have been put to us over the years, but it may answer the question which you as a reader have not had the chance to ask.

The questions normally fall into three categories: religious, mediumship and the spirit world. I will arrange the questions under these headings for the sake of clarity. Our answers are usually given separately, for Jean obviously answers most of the questions on mediumship, I answer the questions related to religion and the philosophy of spiritualism, and we answer jointly on the subject of the spirit world.

RELIGION

Q. *Do you believe in God and Jesus Christ?*

A. Yes, we do. As spiritualists we accept God as our Father. We feel that God's divine power is evident in all living things. Our individual relationship to God is as a child with its parent. We are part of God as He is part of us.

We believe that the life of Jesus was an example to us all. We accept his teachings but adapt them to a modern scientific and questioning audience. Christ was unquestionably a very gifted medium. Examples of his remarkable mediumship and healing are well documented in the Bible.

Q. *Is the service in a spiritualist church very different from the service in an orthodox church?*

A. The obvious difference is a demonstration of clairvoyance. Mediums and speakers such as Jean and myself take the services in spiritualist churches. We have prayers for the sick and for the world. The prayers are not read from a prayer book but are the spontaneous inspirational thoughts received by the medium. There is always a spiritual reading, taken either from the Bible or any other spirit-inspired source.

The service includes a number of hymns sung at various stages throughout. The medium or speaker gives an address on the philosophy of spiritualism or the spirit world, and this can be compared to the sermon in an orthodox church.

The final part of our service is a public demonstration of clairvoyance from the medium. We have spiritualist ministers who hold the same authority as orthodox ministers. You can be married in a spiritualist church, children are baptised and we hold funeral services. All the services offered in orthodox religion are offered in the spiritualist movement.

Q. *Do you still visit other churches?*
A. Yes, we do. As spiritualists we feel that everyone is entitled to follow whatever religious persuasion he or she chooses. No one religion has the monopoly of God's blessing; there are many pathways leading to God and spiritualism is simply one of them. Spiritualism is not dependent on blind faith in our salvation; it offers a rational teaching of our spiritual future. Through the gift of mediumship this spiritual future for us all is proved and demonstrated as a fact.

Q. *I've heard that spiritualism will send you mad. Is this true?*
A. This accusation is made by those who do not understand and are afraid of the growing popularity of spiritualism. These and other stupid remarks stem from fear and ignorance, and come from those who have not investigated the subject or spoken to the right people.

Most of our friends are spiritualists. They are the most normal people you could wish to meet. One of the reasons Jean and I accept and enjoy meetings such as this is to show that we are sensible, rational people. I hope we have proved this point tonight.

Q. *Are there not passages in the Bible that say we should not become involved in such things?*
A. Jean and I are not students of the Bible, and cannot quote

155

chapter and verse as some do. I agree that people use quotations from the Bible that appear to justify their condemnation of spiritualism. The Bible can be interpreted to suit one's own belief or used as a weapon against other religions.

Q. *Do you believe in a heaven and hell?*
A. Not in the concept of being places where we live after death depending on the sort of earthly life we have lived. Heaven and hell are the states of mind we create for ourselves as the result of our own actions and thoughts. We can live in hell during our earthly life. Heaven and hell are our own responsibility, the result of our choice, not the decision of a superior being.

Q. *Some people say mediums work under the influence of the devil. Do you believe in the devil?*
A. We do not believe in the devil as an individual entity. There are of course two separate powers at work in this life and the spirit world, the power for good and the power for evil. Jesus Christ demonstrated his mediumship. Was he working for the devil? When you see the comfort and joy that communication brings to the bereaved and the happiness our work gives to thousands of people you cannot believe that it has anything to do with the devil.

Q. *Do you believe in miracles?*
A. Yes. We feel the miracles of long ago are the spirit phenomena of today.

Q. *How old is spiritualism, and why are orthodox religions so much against it?*
A. Spiritualism is as old as time itself. Communication with spirit has taken place since man walked the earth. Modern-day spiritualism began in 1848, and was introduced into Britain at

the turn of the last century. The first spiritualist church was formed in Keighley in 1853.

I believe that the reason those who practise orthodox religion are against spiritualism is because they can see that spiritualism is offering something, especially to the young, that they seem unable to offer. Many people are becoming dissatisfied with the dogmatic unchanging philosophy of orthodox religion. It is important to stress that spiritualism is not in competition with any other religion; we simply offer an alternative interpretation of God's law.

Q. *Do you believe God helps you in your work?*
A. Yes, totally. I could not work without His help and blessing.

Q. *Have you as a medium ever seen Jesus Christ?*
A. No, just as I never see all the spirit communicators. But as I can sense their presence, so I sense Christ's presence.

Q. *Do you have any doubts about your mediumship or religion?*
A. No.

MEDIUMSHIP

Q. *Is spirit with you all the time?*
A. No. Spirit have their own life to live in the spirit world. They do not hang around me waiting to communicate. Spirit only use me and communicate when there is a reason or need. My friends who work with me from spirit are always close to me, but even they do not make their presence known unless there is just cause.

Q. *Is it possible to communicate with anyone who has passed?*
A. Yes, but only if they *choose* to communicate with me. I am the telephone from spirit; they have to make the call first, and I pass on their message to whoever is on the other end of the line. It is impossible for me to 'call up' any individual. I do not

157

have a directory or direct line to anyone in the spirit world.

Q. *We hear reference to 'spirit guides'. What do they do and why are they usually Red Indian or other exotic nationalities?*
A. We never use the term 'guides'. Spirit are my friends and they work with me from the spirit world in making communication possible. These friends help me in their own individual way according to their own character. I agree that too many mediums say they have this Red Indian or that Chinese guide. I don't. I have an English bank manager, a little girl from Essex, a Scottish lady and a woman who was accused of being a witch. We have checked and proved that these people existed. There are others who work with me who have not yet identified themselves.

Many people who come to see me privately do so because they have problems. How could a Red Indian chief relate to the problems of today? Surely my friends are more used to dealing with today's problems. I know I could not work without their support and help and their organisation.

Q. *Does mediumship ever frighten you?*
A. It did at times, but not any more. I was scared because I didn't know what was happening. Now I have complete control over my mediumship, using it only when I choose or when it is seriously requested. The only time spirit invade my privacy is for very good reasons, usually to offer help or advice to someone in need.

Q. *Has spirit ever told you that someone is going to die?*
A. No. What would it achieve? It would only bring worry and concern. I have had people coming to see me after being told by so-called mediums that someone would die, and they are frightened by this nonsense. I tell them that only God would know this, and He would not deliberately frighten or worry anyone by passing this information on. I have sensed the imminent passing of friends or relatives of sitters whom they

know are very ill and when they are awaiting the inevitable, but that is all. In these circumstances spirit are simply preparing the sitters for something they already know and accept.

Q. *Is there a difference between a medium and a psychic and, if so, are you both?*
A. Yes and yes. A medium has the ability to communicate with the spirit world in various ways. A psychic can sense things about you yourself. Psychics deal with purely materialistic things associated with this life; they do not work with spirit. The information a psychic gives you is what he or she can receive from you. Palmists, fortune tellers, psychometrists, card readers, etc., are all psychics, they are not mediums. At the beginning of a sitting I use psychometry, which is purely a psychic gift I have that tells me about the sitter. I then use my gift of mediumship to link with spirit. My premonitions and predictions are received by psychic means and have nothing to do with spirit. A medium is purely a channel for spirit.

Q. *Why can't everybody see and hear spirit?*
A. Some people are born with the special gift that enables them to see or hear spirit, or both. I was one of these lucky people. A medium is born with the gift; it cannot be acquired or learnt. If you have the gift, it can be developed and controlled.

Q. *I have seen and spoken to my father who has passed. Does that mean I'm a medium?*
A. No. A medium is someone who has been trained to act as the intermediary between this world and the spirit world and so pass information and messages to others. From what you have said it is possible that you may have the potential to become a medium, but we would have to assess your potential in a development class. The first thing we would do through a series of exercises would be to make sure it wasn't your imagination.

Q. *There seem to be more women mediums than men. Why is this?*
A. Actually we know as many men as women who are mediums, but you are probably correct. I feel it may be because women are by nature more sensitive than men. They are therefore more likely to be aware of this faculty within themselves and so accept it more readily. A very good word used to describe a medium is a 'sensitive', for that is exactly what we are: very sensitive people.

Q. *How do you see spirit, and what can you see?*
A. I see spirit in various ways. At times I can see them as clearly and as solidly as I can see you and you can see me. It is as if I am looking at a physical person, and sometimes I think I am until they suddenly disappear. More commonly I see a picture in my mind of the spirit and can describe them precisely and accurately from this impression. Sometimes I see what one might think of as a ghost, a vague image that appears transparent, as if seeing someone through a thick mist. Another very common way spirit show themselves to me is purely by a feeling. This feeling is so powerful that I am able to describe the spirit solely on the strength of it.

The clarity of spirit's presence and my vision depends very much on atmosphere and conditions. This is not an excuse used by mediums if their demonstration is not very good; conditions do play a vital part in successful communication.

Q. *How do you hear spirit talking to you?*
A. Again I hear spirit in various ways. I can hear spirit as clear and as loud as I hear your voice. Sometimes it is just a voice in my head, but I know it is not my own thoughts for the voice in my mind is not my own. Often they simply give me thoughts to pass on and I don't hear a voice at all.

Q. *Can you tell if a person has the gift or not?*
A. Yes. A medium can sense the presence of another medium.

Q. *Do your guides – sorry, your friends – stay with you all your life?*
A. Yes.

Q. *How long does it take to train a medium?*
A. For ever. Mediums never finish their training. We train mediums until we are satisfied that they are ready to take a public platform, then we tell them their development will continue between themselves and their friends in spirit.

Mediums should always be refining and improving their gift. They should never cease striving with spirit's help to perfect and improve communication. They should never feel satisfied with their efforts, for satisfaction leads to complacency. There is always room for improvement in content and presentation. The perfect message has yet to be given. As long as there is any doubt about the authenticity of mediumship, all mediums need to continue seeking perfection.

Q. *Who would you say is the best medium?*
A. No such person exists. There are some mediums who have developed their mediumship to a higher degree than others and are obviously more dedicated. I personally strive for the highest standard possible as a token of respect for my spirit friends, and I expect and demand the same from them. Together we do quite well but we still have a long way to go.

Q. *How quickly after death have you spoken to someone?*
A. I have spoken with spirit before the physical body has been buried or cremated. There is no time limit on when communication can take place. It could be the instant a person passes or it could be many years afterwards that they choose to communicate. I have found that it is more common to receive a communication early after passing from someone who accepted life after death than from someone who was very sceptical. But there is no time-scale that regulates communication.

Q. *Why do spirit choose you to communicate through?*
A. Because I am available at that time. Spirit are aware of my ability, and when I am in the presence of their relatives or friends, whether at a public meeting or a private sitting, and open the door to them, they use the opportunity to relay messages to their relatives. They have to use me because they know their relatives do not have the ability to receive their messages themselves.

Q. *Of all the people in spirit you have met, who has been in spirit the longest?*
A. That is very difficult to answer when you consider that I have been in touch with spirit most of my life. I can only say that in some cases it was a person who had been there for hundreds of years. Spirit do not relate to time as we do, so the time-lapse is not noticeable to them.

Q. *You have mentioned the protection you receive from Henry and your other spirit friends. Do they shield you from problems?*
A. I'm glad you asked that. Many people have said that because I work for spirit and have their protection I must never have problems. My spirit friends protect me from the unpleasant influences that exist in the spirit world, but that's all they do. They cannot interfere in our ordinary life. Spirit share my life with me; they do not rule it. I have exactly the same difficulties over family, money and all the other problems that arise in modern-day living. I keep telling everyone I'm not special in any way; I was simply born with special gifts, that's all.

Q. *Can you inherit mediumship?*
A. Yes. My grandmother had the gift, yet neither of my parents has shown any sign of mediumship. In my case it appears to have skipped a generation.

Q. *My young son talks to a friend every day. Neither I nor my husband can see or hear his friend. Could he be talking to a spirit friend?*

A. Yes, indeed he could, and how lovely. Please don't try to stop your son talking to his friend. Most children are aware of spirit and make friends with spirit children. It is only when adults or parents ridicule or plant a seed of doubt in the child's mind that this natural friendship ceases. Join in your son's relationship, ask questions about his friend. You may be very surprised at the outcome. Some children do conjure up imaginary friends, but in most cases they really do exist. So please don't think your son is strange; I assure you he is not.

Q. *Surely the messages you give people could be pure telepathy on your part?*

A. Telepathy is a very important part of mediumship. Many of the messages I get from spirit are received telepathically. Spirit direct their thoughts to me and I pass them on to the sitter. When I pass on information from spirit that the sitters cannot know, or that they will have to go away and check, and when that information is proved correct, how can that be telepathy? You can only receive from the sitter what the sitter wants you to receive. Sitters cannot give you what they themselves don't know.

Q. *How can I tell if a medium is genuine or not?*

A. Simply use your common sense. Evaluate what is said and assess the evidence you are given. Don't accept anything that could apply to anyone, question what you don't understand or cannot accept, never be afraid to say no. Record the sitting and play it to someone who can also pass a rational judgement. Nothing weird or unusual should ever happen during a private sitting with a genuine medium. The medium will simply sit and talk to you in his or her own voice. Be very suspicious of so-called 'trance' messages.

If after your sitting you are dissatisfied with what has taken place, simply refuse to pay the fee. Never pay before the sitting.

163

You should be in no doubt at the end of the sitting whether the medium has been in contact with spirit or not.

Q. *How do you know whom you are going to speak to at a large public meeting?*
A. That's a very interesting and popular question. All mediums work in their own way, one that has been practised and agreed with their spirit friends. A medium must feel happy in his or her technique of communication and identification. I spent many years experimenting with Henry in various ways of identifying whom we should be talking to at public demonstrations. We now use two methods, depending on how many people are present. If there are too many for me to see everybody, Henry directs me by a feeling of being drawn to a particular area of the hall. I begin the message and wait for the response from that area. If more than one person accepts the first part of the message, I ask Henry to get some information from spirit to identify the one person in the audience. This usually comes immediately and then we proceed with the message. If the audience is small enough for me to see everybody, then as spirit draw close their faces slowly go out of focus until there is only one face in the audience I can see clearly. I know then that that is the person to whom spirit wish to speak. It's not foolproof and we have got it wrong on rare occasions, but in the main it works well.

Q. *Have you ever seen into the future?*
A. Yes, usually in the case of a tragic accident or misfortune. It's what we call precognition or premonition, and I cannot offer any explanation of how or why it happens. I know it is not information I receive from spirit. I wish that I didn't get this information, and thankfully it is not very common.

Q. *Do you perform exorcisms as in the film* The Exorcist?
A. No, I do not perform exorcisms. People do call upon my services as a medium if they are having disturbances in their

homes, but I do not exorcise the spirit, I try to help them. We call this 'rescue work'.

Q. *Has being a medium changed your way of thinking about life?*
A. My attitudes have changed considerably. Two things spring to mind whenever I am asked this question. First, because of the years of receiving communication from spirit I have completely lost my fear of death. I know we will all live on in the spirit world, and if we choose we can continue to give love, comfort and advice to loved ones we have left behind. The second thing I have learnt from being a medium is that if there is something we have asked for or hoped for in life which has not yet materialised, there are two reasons: either the time is not yet right or we haven't earned the reward. I have learnt that we receive from life according to the effort we put into it.

Q. *Do you ever feel special or important as a medium on a platform in public?*
A. I have never felt important and I hope I never do. Special? Perhaps, but it's my gifts that are special and they were given to me to help others. I feel privileged to have been given these gifts and I try not to allow them to make me feel any more important than anyone else. We all have our own special gifts and hopefully we recognise and use them. Mine are just a little more rare, that's all.

Q. *If you had the choice, would you rather be an 'ordinary' person or would you rather be a medium?*
A. I'd stay exactly as I am now, an 'ordinary medium'.

THE SPIRIT WORLD
Q. *There must be millions of people in the spirit world. Isn't it crowded?*
A. No. The spirit is not a physical body, therefore it does not

165

occupy a physical space. There are probably hundreds of spirit friends here with us this evening, yet we do not feel crowded. The world of spirit is not a physical place like the earth, it is a conscious state of the soul without the limitations of physical boundaries.

Q. *What happens to babies or children when they pass to spirit?*
A. They continue to grow in the spirit world. In this life a child grows physically and mentally, gaining knowledge and maturity. In spirit the growth continues but without the physical stages. Jean has often described to parents their son or daughter who passed as a baby or a young child, but the description is of a young man or woman corresponding to the age they would have attained had they lived a physical life. Spirit manifest in this guise purely so that the relative can see and relate to the growth of their child. The obvious sign of the growth of a child is its physical appearance, and spirit use this physical indication of growth to demonstrate the evidence of growth in the spirit world. (The picture we have of Lucy, Jean's spirit friend, is not that of a six-year-old girl, but as she would have looked at the time the portrait was drawn had she lived on in this life. Proof of this was given in *More To Life Than This*.)

Q. *Why did you describe my father as a much younger man than he was when he died?*
A. You accepted that the description fitted exactly how your father looked at that age. Spirit, as the previous answer shows, can manifest themselves to us as they wish. It is very common for spirit to show themselves to me as they would have appeared at the happiest time of their earthly life. Surely this is how you would wish to remember your loved ones, not as very sick and unhappy people. Spirit also want you to remember them in the happy times, so they appear to me as they were then.

Q. *You have said that someone severely handicapped in the physical body does not have the disability in spirit. Why then do mediums describe their physical disabilities?*

A. It is a fact that physical disability is left behind with the death of the physical body. I have described many physical handicaps that spirit have shown me they had on earth. They do this in the beginning purely so that the relative may recognise their presence. Once they have been recognised I see them change to the healthy, happy and complete spirit. I always quickly explain that their loved one is no longer handicapped but is now happy and well.

Q. *Do animals pass to the spirit world?*

A. Yes, they do. Animals also have a spirit that lives on as we do in the spirit world. They too are reunited with their owners, as we are reunited with our loved ones. In the many messages I have conveyed from relatives in the spirit world I have often described their pets who are with them. This always gives great comfort to sitters. There is a plane in spirit where animals live in peace and happiness with each other.

Q. *Do you eat and sleep in spirit?*

A. This depends on the spiritual progress and understanding of the individual. Having passed from a life where food and sleep were a daily necessity, it can be difficult to adjust to a life that does not require food or sleep. At first many who pass to spirit still cling to their earthly habits, eating and drinking. In spirit what you think, is. If you think of food and drink strongly enough, you have it. I have given messages from spirit who say, 'It's great here – all the drinks are free.' The realisation soon comes that the spirit does not require food and the need fades away.

As to sleep, spirit do rest but it's not a loss of consciousness as in normal sleep. They move into a much deeper spiritual environment which recharges and energises the spirit.

Q. *Can you make love in the spirit world?*
A. A very good and popular question. The physical act of making love should be the expression of love from one person to another. In spirit the ability to express and demonstrate one's love to another continues, but is achieved by the joining and bonding of the spirit. Even in our earthly life we can feel as close to another human being in a spiritual as in a physical relationship, and in many cases even closer. If you are fortunate to have this emotional and spiritual relationship with a fellow human being, imagine the situation magnified a thousand times in a purely spiritual environment between two or more pure free spirits – then you may begin to understand the meaning of spiritual intercourse.

Is it not a fact that a spiritual relationship is far more meaningful and fulfilling and more likely to stand the test of time than a purely physical one? I can see some heads shaking in disagreement, and when I was younger my head would probably have been shaking as well, but believe me it is true and I hope you will find it so through personal experience.

Q. *I have been married twice. Will I meet both husbands when I pass to spirit?*
A. Whom you meet in the spirit world will depend on the type of relationship you had with that person during your earthly life. If you sincerely loved both husbands and they loved you, then there will be no jealousy between you: it will be a joining and blending of spiritual love for each other described in the previous answer.

Q. *What is spirit?*
A. Spirit is another word used to describe the soul. In the spirit world your spirit continues its eternal life. The spirit lives on in another dimension that we call the spirit world. Your spirit is a duplicate or extension of you, removed from the restrictions of a physical body. Your spirit cannot be destroyed; it can never die.

Q. *Do you believe in reincarnation?*
A. It makes sense to me, and I would like to think it is possible that we have the opportunity to return in another life to gain further experience and understanding. I feel, however, that it has yet to be proved beyond doubt. Reincarnation and spirit communication are both fascinating subjects and we are gaining knowledge all the time on both, but there is still so much unknown. One day we may get all the answers but that day is a long way off.

Q. *Do we grow old and die again in the spirit world?*
A. It is only the physical body that ages because it is related to physical environments and time. The spirit and the spirit world are not governed or influenced by time. Time itself is purely a measure of experience. There is a constant progression of the spirit that cannot be measured in hours, days or years; it is eternal and eternity is timeless. We do move to higher planes in the spirit world according to our spiritual development. This transition from one plane to another could be described as new rebirths, but never as death, for the spirit cannot die.

Q. *When does a physical body receive the spirit?*
A. At conception.

Q. *If what you say is correct, how do you feel about abortion?*
A. This is a difficult and very emotive question. Thank God I have never been called upon to make such a serious decision. There are so many factors that come into the question of abortion – spiritual, moral, physical and mental, to name a few. I can only reply that it is a very personal decision made by the individual and obviously depends on the circumstances surrounding each particular case. I feel that it is impossible to generalise on such a question.

Q. *What happens in the case of a miscarriage?*
A. There are occasions when owing to physical accidents the

foetus does not develop as it should and is rejected by the physical body. The spirit then returns to its source and begins its progression in the spirit world. We refer to this as a 'pure spirit'. We have been told by spirit friends that there are occasions when the spirit that could not remain in an imperfect foetus does return to the next conception and lives an earthly life in the new physical body. This philosophy you will understand is based on information from spirit friends and must be speculative, as it is virtually impossible to prove.

Q. *I lost a baby before he was born. How will I recognise him when we meet in the spirit world?*
A. I'm so pleased you know that you and your son will meet in the spirit world. Your physical awareness may not recognise or relate to a baby that did not achieve full development and eventual natural birth, but your spirit will, and when the time comes and you link in the spirit world the recognition and love between you will be instant and undeniable. Believe me, you will immediately know your son, and the relationship that has continued through your physical life, which you may not have been aware of, will be confirmed and will then continue in the spirit world.

Q. *Will other relatives be there to meet me when I pass?*
A. Yes. The love and nearness of loved ones continue. They will want to help you and greet you on your transition to spirit. This is a time of reunion.

Q. *Do you continue to work in spirit?*
A. Yes, indeed. Wouldn't it be a boring place if we all just sat about doing nothing for eternity? Spiritual healing is one example of spirit continuing their work from the spirit world. People who in their earthly life helped relieve pain and suffering work through spiritual healers to continue their mission from spirit. I know that many people in all walks of life and in all sorts of different work receive inspiration and guidance from

spirit friends, who are continuing their various callings from the spirit world.

Q. *Are we ever punished in the spirit world?*
A. No. There is no judgement by a superior being for our shortcomings or sins. We ourselves are fully aware of our own sins, and with repentance we strive to bring our own redemption and recompense. We find a state of humility and forgiveness within ourselves. We are our own judge and jury, and answer to ourselves for our thoughts and deeds towards others in our earthly life.

Q. *Can we go where we like in spirit, and meet whom we choose?*
A. Yes, depending on our spiritual affinity with others. Like attracts like: if you feel this affinity with someone who has passed to spirit, there is no reason why you cannot meet that person. Status or position in earthly life has no importance in spirit. There are no class barriers in the spirit world. Physical death is a great leveller. We *all* leave this world without our worldly possessions; the only thing we take with us to the spirit world is our spirit.

Q. *I hate to think of my friends among the nasty people in the spirit world. Is this possible?*
A. No. Your friends would not have associated with these types in their earthly life, so why should they choose to mix with them in spirit? Your loved ones are with those they choose to be with in the spirit world. Remember, 'Like attracts like.'

Q. *Will you meet Henry and Lucy when you go to spirit?*
A. Yes, definitely. They have told me we will meet very quickly when I pass. I am really looking forward to meeting all my spirit friends 'in the flesh', as you might say.

Q. *Is it possible to visit the spirit world before we die?*
A. Yes. The spirit can separate itself from the physical body

during our earthly life and travel over any distance, then it will return. This phenomenon is called 'astral travelling' or 'out of the body' experiences. Many people during serious illness, for example, have described the experience of looking down on their physical body that is still lying in bed. This is the conscious awareness of the separation of the spirit and physical body. Such separation is more common than we realise. In most cases it takes place as we sleep and we are not aware that it has happened. We talk of having a vivid dream and meeting people who seemed 'so real'. Because the spirit can travel wherever it chooses it can obviously visit the world of spirit. The problem is that most of us cannot remember the experience or are not conscious of it. Many of these experiences are stored in the subconscious part of our mind and may never rise to the normal consciousness.

Q. *I feel it would be a very frightening experience to see a relative who I knew had died standing at the foot of my bed. Can you reassure me?*
A. It is quite understandable to think it would be a frightening experience, but I can assure you that it would not be. All the people who have had this experience – I mean 'ordinary' people who have not trained as mediums etc. – have said that it was a marvellous feeling and they never felt at all frightened. Do you really think that a loved one would do anything he or she knew would harm or frighten you? I speak from years of experience in saying how comforting it is to see and know how close a loved one is to you. However, I am glad in one way that you feel the way you do, for it shows me that you will never play about in communication with spirit, and that you will not become involved in the wrong way just for fun, as some do.

Q. *Can spirit ever hurt us?*
A. Spirit have the power to influence a person's mind, so depending on the motive or personality of the spirit the influ-

ence could be harmful. If the influence were malevolent, I could accept that the person might get hurt.

Q. *What advice would you give anyone who is genuinely interested?*
A. Seek the advice of a professional medium. Join a discussion group and ask questions at every opportunity. Go along to various spiritualist churches, but always keep an open mind on what you may see or hear. Use your common sense and be prepared to disregard the rubbish. In time you will find what you require, but be patient and determined – and good luck to you.

These questions are just a sample of the hundreds of questions people ask on the subject. The answers we gave are the result of years of investigation and communication with spirit. If ever you are invited into a development group, use the communication with spirit to ask your questions. Spirit enjoy the chance to educate and enlighten us when they can sense a genuinely interested and inquisitive person. The more involved one becomes the more one is aware of just how little we really know. As the striving for knowledge and understanding increases it becomes like an unquenchable thirst. It will change your whole way of life. To find the answer to the question man has asked since creation, 'What *will* happen to me when I die?', is immeasurably rewarding and comforting, and will prove to you that your efforts were justified.

One final comment that often arises at our meetings will serve to express the feeling of many.

I have sat through the whole meeting, I have listened to the talk and seen Jean give her demonstration. I have listened to the questions and your answers, but still I believe it's all a load of rubbish.

Good for you, we feel pleased. You are very honest and not afraid to voice your opinion openly. It proves you are not easily persuaded and have a questioning mind. Jean and I have never attempted to convert anyone to our way of life or understanding. We have received so much evidence that has proved to us that there *is* life after death. We *know* that communication with spirit is a fact; we do not *believe* that spirit exist, we have proved it.

You are entitled to your opinion – and remember, I once shared exactly the same attitude. Tonight you will have seen how my deep scepticism has changed. This change took many years and was not easy in coming. If you pass to spirit before I do, I will expect your apology from spirit through Jean. If I pass first, then you can apologise at our first meeting in the spirit world. Whatever happens, I know I will receive your apology one way or the other. Until then God bless you.